CREATE STUNNING LARGE-SCALE WALL ART, HEADBOARDS, BACKDROPS
AND PLANT HANGERS WITH STEP-BY-STEP TUTORIALS

STATEMENT
macramé

natalie ranae

MACRAMÉ ARTIST AND INSTRUCTOR,
AUTHOR OF *MACRAMÉ AT HOME*

PAGE STREET
PUBLISHING CO.

PAGE STREET
PUBLISHING CO.

First published in 2020 by

Page Street Publishing Co.

27 Congress Street, Suite 105

Salem, MA 01970

www.pagestreetpublishing.com

Distributed by Macmillan, sales in Canada by The Canadian Manda Group.

24 23 22 21 20   1 2 3 4 5

ISBN-13: 978-1-64567-007-0

ISBN-10: 1-64567-007-4

Library of Congress Control Number: 2019951501

Cover and book design by Meg Baskis for Page Street Publishing Co.

Photography by Jennifer Cornthwaite of Jennifer See Studios

Printed and bound in the United States

dedication

TO EVERYONE WHO SUPPORTED MY FIRST BOOK.
AND TO THE LOVE OF MY LIFE, THE MAN I WOULD
NEVER WANT TO LIVE WITHOUT: SHAWN.

contents

INTRODUCTION

I truly love working on large pieces of macramé. The satisfaction you get when you finally take a step back and look at what you created with your own two hands is worth all the hard work! Whenever I finish a new large-scale macramé piece, I feel happy knowing that I challenged myself in a new way and learned more from the process. Turning something as ordinary as rope into a beautiful and interesting design on an impressively large scale is just so satisfying.

Over the last few years I've taught a lot of introductory macramé workshops to hundreds of students, and in every single class I've noticed that many people were there because they aspired to make large-scale pieces. However, I would also have many people messaging me later to ask for help tackling these big projects with questions like, "How long should my initial rope lengths be?" or "How do I even get started planning a big piece of macramé?" Creating large-scale or statement macramé pieces is somewhat of an art form in and of itself, because it comes with a unique set of challenges and concepts that you might not encounter while making a small wall hanging or plant hanger. After many years of experience, I have figured out some techniques, tips and tricks that work well for me, and I'm so excited to share them with you in this book!

I've been fortunate to have the opportunity to create a variety of large macramé pieces for a number of different purposes. I've taken that experience and channeled it into twelve large projects in this book that can be used in homes, for special events like weddings and parties, and anywhere else you can dream up!

This book contains projects that suit different styles and skill levels, from intermediate to expert. If you already know a few macramé knots and have experience creating a small macramé wall hanging or plant hanger, then this is the book for you! However, if you're completely new to macramé, you can still make these pieces, as I have included instructions for every knot in the Knots and Patterns Guide on page 126. Just keep in mind that you may find things to be a bit more challenging at the beginning, as there will be a steeper learning curve. I'm confident that you'll succeed if you give yourself the time and take things step by step, but if you still find yourself having trouble with the projects in this book, then I'd recommend picking up a copy of my first book, *Macramé at Home*, which contains some smaller projects specifically designed for beginners.

I am so excited for you to dive into this book, and I can't wait to see your completed projects! If you post any photos on social media, please tag me so that I can see your beautiful creations! You can find me mostly on Instagram at @natalie_ranae and sometimes on Facebook at facebook.com/natalieranaehome.

have questions?

Community can be so helpful! If you ever feel stuck or have a question about a project or instruction in this book, chances are someone else might have had the same question! I always do my best to try and answer any questions, but since I am only one person I thought it would be helpful to create a Facebook group where you can post and ask questions about this book (and my last one, *Macramé at Home*)! If you are interested in joining this group, just search "Natalie Ranae Macramé Book Community" on Facebook and request to join!

Please respect that all of the projects and instructions in this book are my original designs. I've created them for your personal use and kindly request that you not sell the finished products. Thank you so much for respecting my work in this way!

GETTING STARTED MAKING LARGE-SCALE MACRAMÉ

GETTING SET UP

My typical setup when working on macramé is an adjustable clothing rack on wheels with two S hooks that hang from the rack and hold the piece. How you work on larger-scale projects really depends on the size of the piece. You'll be surprised at how much you can do on one of these clothing racks, and you can even use two or three racks lined up next to each other to support a really long piece.

Another option that I find helpful and inexpensive is using two long wall brackets designed for shelves or hanging plants. I attach them to the wall at the desired height and around 7 feet (2.1 m) or so apart and place a thick wood dowel around 8 feet (2.5 m) in length across the two brackets. I then hang the piece of macramé from S hooks, or two strings tied at incremental heights. Another setup I've used in a larger studio space is a canoe hoist pulley system typically designed for use in garages. This worked incredibly well as I could adjust the hanging height really easily and it could support the weight of a large piece, which is something you should consider when working on the projects in this book. The weight of rope can add up quickly, so keep that in mind for whatever setup you're using. Any of these setups work for alternating between standing and sitting.

BEFORE YOU START

I use a measuring tape, scissors and masking tape for every project in this book, so these won't be listed in the tools or materials section. Make sure you have them for each project. I use masking tape on the ends of most of my cords, to keep the rope from unraveling while I work.

Cut and prep most or all of your rope before starting. It's like batch working—most of the time it's easier and faster to do it all at once when you're already set up and in the flow of prepping. It can be helpful to hang the cords in half from an S hook to keep them organized. In a pinch, I'll lay them out on the floor in rows.

I like to put a dowel through the hole of the spool of rope and put that through a milk crate or over a large storage bin. This allows the spools to freely spin while cutting the rope lengths. Secure the ends of your rope by placing a piece of masking tape around the rope and cutting in the middle of the tape. This will help keep the rope from unraveling when you're pulling the cords through each knot.

KNOT TIPS FOR WORKING LARGE

Bundle your cords when they're really long (page 158). I personally only do this when the cords are too long to work with. If it only takes a couple of pulls to work the rope through a knot, then I would rather let them pile on the floor and leave them unbundled.

Make sure you tie the knots the easier way depending on the rope lengths. Check to see if there are any helpful hits in the Knots and Patterns Guide (page 126) for certain knots you're working with. This can save you a lot of time! See, for example, the double half hitch method on page 132. Even though you may know how to tie some of these knots already, I think it's worth checking each knot's tutorial for any project you're working on to make sure you know the best practices and tricks!

Everyone ties their knots and keeps their tension between knots a little differently. This could affect the rope lengths needed for a project. Though I have built in a little buffer room in each project, it could be helpful to add an extra foot (30 cm) or so to each rope length to account for any differences. If you're new to macramé, you should consider practicing these knots before tackling your first project.

Take breaks and stretch. Macramé is deceptively hard on your body and involves a lot of repetitive movements! Since I do this full-time, I see my massage therapist and chiropractor regularly. Make sure to take care of your body!

FIGURING OUT THE WEIGHT OF A LARGE MACRAMÉ PIECE

When it comes time to hang a finished large piece of macramé, it is important to consider the weight of it before deciding how to hang it. Macramé can be deceptively heavy, and you would never want it to fall and break or hurt someone! The simplest way to figure out its weight is to hold it while standing on a bathroom scale. Then subtract your body weight from the total weight. Once you know how much it weighs, you can choose the right method for hanging and the appropriate screws and drywall anchors. See page 20 for my method for installing wall hangings.

USE LEFTOVER OR SCRAP ROPE

Use leftover or scrap rope whenever possible. This can be helpful when making things like a fringe overlay and can save you a lot of money and significantly reduce your waste, as done with the Annalise Backdrop (page 89). It's inevitable that you'll have leftover rope, even if you try your best to avoid it.

Here are some ideas for making use of this rope so it doesn't go to waste: use it for fringes, tassels and tufting, make mini wall hangings or send it to someone to process and spin it into repurposed yarn. I save A LOT of rope to use on future projects, and it has saved me from having to buy new rope on so many occasions!

USEFUL TERMS AND PHRASES

Working cords: When tying a knot, these are the cords you are handling and physically using to tie the knot. For example, the working cords are the two cords on the outside of four cords used to tie a square knot (page 130).

Filler cords: These are the cords that knots are being tied around. They are typically the cords in the middle of the knots. For example, the two filler cords are in the middle of a square knot (page 130).

"Tight to the row/knots before": This phrase refers to the space left between each row or knot and is indicating for you to leave no space. This means the knots row after row are tied with no space in between each knot and row.

"Vs or Upside-down/inverted Vs": This refers to a shape created by the knots in a specific pattern that resembles the shape of an upright V or upside-down V. It's an easier way to reference parts throughout a project (page 155).

Fringe: The frayed unraveled rope usually at the bottom of the piece (page 159).

Unravel: This refers to undoing a piece of rope. See my method for unraveling rope on page 158.

Gap: This refers to leaving a specified amount of space between two rows or knots.

headboards
& WALL HANGINGS

Macramé wall hangings and headboards make for great focal points and elevate any space they occupy. They're quite often one of the first things people notice in a room, so I'm certain you'll be fielding a lot of compliments about these projects, wherever you choose to display them.

A macramé headboard is the only large-scale piece that has been permanently hanging in my house over the last few years. It has stayed above my bed all this time because it is visually interesting and complex, yet also delicate, soft to the touch and inviting. It's also the statement macramé piece that I've received the most questions about from makers, so I'm happy to finally share instructions here to help you create one or two for yourself!

There's a wide variety of styles in this chapter because I wanted to create unique designs that could fit with different looks. From geometric to boho, there's something in here for everyone.

HARVEST HEADBOARD

There's something about a macramé headboard that everyone seems to love, myself included! I thought it was about time I created a unique design for you to make and hang in your own home! I love the striking geometric pattern the rope creates. Macramé brings such a warm textural element to a space, which I especially love in a bedroom. It's the perfect focal point above the bed and gives that irresistible boho-chic charm you're looking for!

Tip: If you would like to make it wider (width wise) before starting, simply get a longer dowel, cut 10, 20 or 30 more cords (working in sections of 10 to expand the pine tree pattern properly) of ³⁄₁₆-inch (5-mm) three-strand rope, each 108 inches (274 cm) long, and add them to the dowel following the same pattern.

skill level: intermediate

DIMENSIONS
59½ inches (151 cm) wide x 15 inches (38 cm) high

MATERIALS AND TOOLS
About 566 feet (173 m) of ³⁄₁₆-inch (5-mm) three-strand rope

1 wooden dowel 70 inches (178 cm) long

About 46 feet (14 m) of ¹⁄₁₆-inch (1.5-mm) three-strand rope

Large-eye needle

Screws for hanging

KNOTS USED
Lark's Head Knot (page 127)

Horizontal Double Half Hitch (page 151)

Alternating Square Knot (page 143)

Square Knot (page 130)

Pine Tree Pattern (page 142)

Double Half Hitch (page 132)

Overhand Knot (page 134)

1. Cut 60 pieces of ³⁄₁₆-inch (5-mm) three-strand rope, each 108 inches (274 cm) long. Fold each piece in half and attach to the dowel with a lark's head knot. When attaching the rope, position the cords so each cord is just slightly touching each other, leaving 6¼ inches (16 cm) of empty wooden dowel on both sides.

   Then cut 4 pieces of ³⁄₁₆-inch (5-mm) three-strand rope, each 78 inches (198 cm) long.

2. Tie 120 horizontal double half hitches, with every cord, around 1 of the 78-inch (198-cm)-long pieces of rope, acting as the filler cord. Make sure to tie the double half hitches tight to the lark's head knots above. Leave about a 7-inch (17.5-cm) tail on both sides on the filler cord.

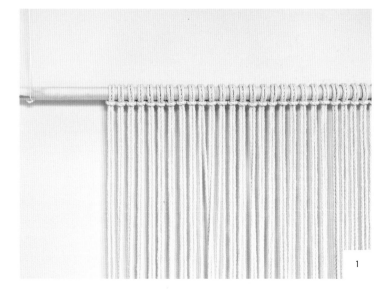

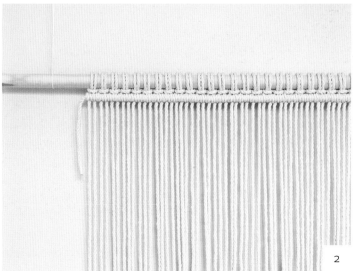

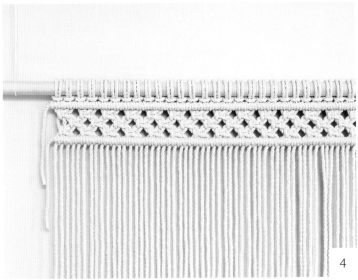

3. Tie 3 rows of alternating square knots, tight to the row above. Be sure to tie the square knot rows tight to each other, leaving no space between each knot.

4. Tie 120 horizontal double half hitches, with every cord, around 1 more of the cut 78-inch (198-cm)-long pieces of rope, acting as the filler cord. Make sure to tie the double half hitches tight to the row above. Leave about a 7-inch (17.5-cm) tail on both sides on the filler cord.

5. Counting 8 cords over, using the next 4 adjacent cords to the right, tie one square knot tight to the row above.

6. Using the first cord on either side of the square knot you just tied as your new working cords, tie a square knot around the same filler cords from your previous square knot. Leave the previous square knots' working cords hanging behind. You will have a square knot tied directly underneath the previous.

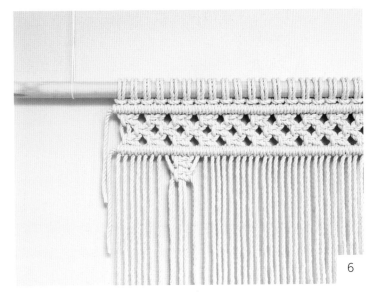

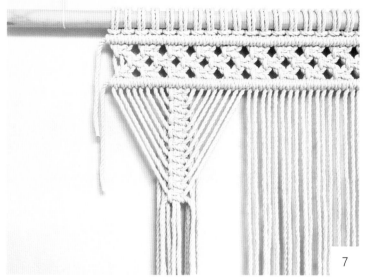

7

8

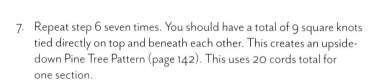

7. Repeat step 6 seven times. You should have a total of 9 square knots tied directly on top and beneath each other. This creates an upside-down Pine Tree Pattern (page 142). This uses 20 cords total for one section.

8. Repeat steps 5 through 7 six times. You should end up with 7 upside-down pine trees next to each other.

9. Take 1 more of the cut 78-inch (198-cm)-long pieces of rope to use as a filler cord for this step. Using the corresponding working cords left hanging behind from step 7 (working from the top square knot working cords to the bottom), tie 1 double half hitch with the first cord. Make sure to leave a 7-inch (17.5-cm) tail before tying your first double half hitch. Try to line up your first double half hitch knot so that it will be directly under the last square knot from step 7. Do this by holding the double half hitch knot even with the double half hitch above, from step 4. Adjust your first double half hitch knot accordingly. If you are having trouble lining up the double half hitch, it may be easier to do this step with the wall hanging lying on the floor.

10. Using the second corresponding working cord from step 6's second square knot, tie another double half hitch next to the one you just tied.

9

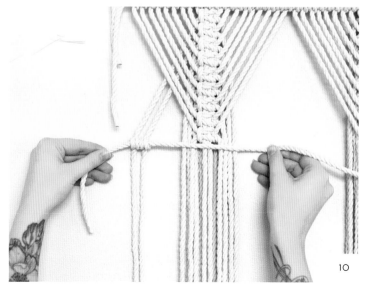

10

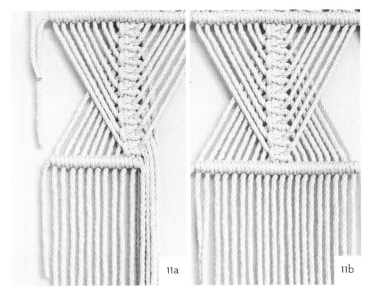

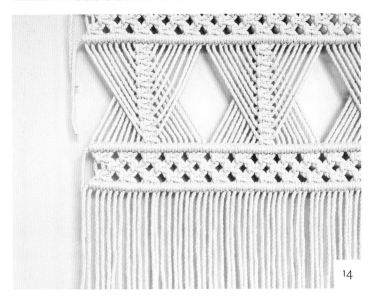

11. Tie 8 more horizontal double half hitches, using every corresponding working cord from step 7. Adjust the height of your knots so the row aligns right under the square knot. Tie 10 more horizontal double half hitches, being mindful of keeping the row at the same height.

12. Continue tying horizontal double half hitches until you get to the end of the row. You should have a total of 120 double half hitches. There should be an approximate 7-inch (17.5-cm) tail on the filler cord.

13. Tie 3 rows of alternating square knots, tight to the row above. Be sure to tie the square knot rows tight to each other, leaving no space between each knot.

14. Tie 120 horizontal double half hitches, with every cord, around the last 78-inch (198-cm)-long piece of rope, acting as the filler cord. Make sure to tie the double half hitches tight to the row above. Leave about a 7-inch (17.5-cm) tail on both sides on the filler cord.

15

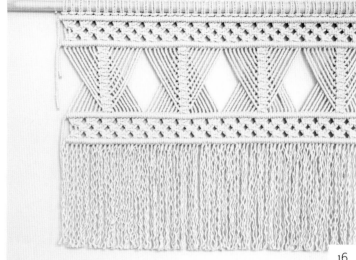

16

17

15. Trim the hanging cords to approximately 10 inches (25.5 cm) long (or your preferred length), measuring from the last double half hitch row. It's OK if some of your cords are shorter than 10 inches (25.5 cm).

16. Unravel each cord to create the fringe. Follow my method on page 158 to get a full-looking fringe for three-strand rope.

17. To create the alternating tassels: Cut 69 pieces of 1/16-inch (1.5-mm) three-strand rope, each 8 inches (20 cm) long. Gathering 12 strands of unraveled rope together, wrap 1 of the 8-inch (20-cm)-long pieces of rope around the gathered strands, 3 times. Make sure to wrap the strands tight to the row of double half hitches above. Secure the wrap by tying an overhand knot, with the ends at the back of the wall hanging. Repeat 35 times, so you have tied 36 tassels all the way across the length of the wall hanging. Reference the photo from step 19 to see the back of these knots.

18. To start the second row of tassels, leave 6 strands of unraveled rope to hang at the very edge of both sides of the wall hanging. Gather 12 strands of unraveled rope together, 6 strands from the one tassel above and 6 strands from the other tassel above, leaving about 1 inch (2.5 cm) of space from the row of wrapped tassels above, and tie it the same way, all the way across the wall hanging. Repeat 34 times, leaving 6 strands at the end of the row to hang. Feel free to leave this step out if you prefer it without the tassels—it looks good either way! If you do, you can skip to step 19.

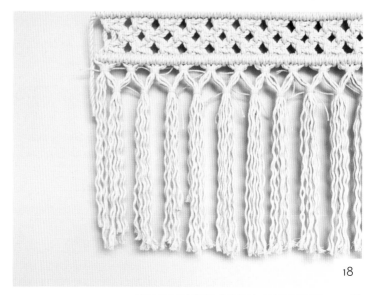

18

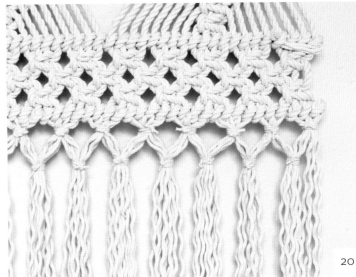

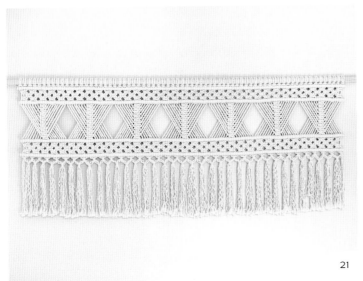

19. Turn the wall hanging around for convenience (so that you are looking at the back). Unravel the ends of the filler cords from the double half hitch rows from steps 2, 4, 12 and 14. Using a large-eye needle, sew the unraveled ends into the back of the fourth double half hitch from the end. Repeat this with each of the filler cords from the double half hitches, on both sides of the wall hanging.

20. Trim the excess cords that you sewed into the back close to the double half hitch. Trim the ends of the 1⁄16-inch (1.5-mm) cord that you used to wrap the tassels close to the knot.

21. Give a final trim to the fringe if desired. You are finished with your wall hanging! Hang above your bed (or anywhere) and enjoy.

hanging Tips:

I like to hang mine with two long screws anchored in studs (or drywall anchors that can support the weight) and place the dowel on top of the two screws. To slightly hide the screws, place the screws in between the lark's head knots or where the lark's head knots can cover the screws, so you don't see them at all!

My piece weighed 4.2 pounds (2 kg), but to be safe you should always weigh your own finished piece. See page 10 for an easy way to weigh large macramé pieces.

Note that if you make any adjustments to the project, it may change the weight.

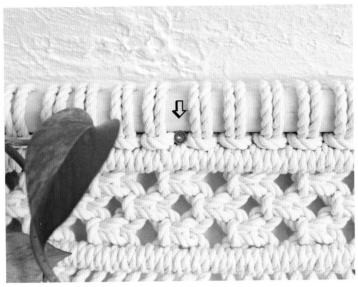

LUNA WALL HANGING

I absolutely love mixed media art. I think macramé lends itself well to being used alongside other mediums because its soft and fibrous nature complements strong and solid materials like wood. In this project, the wood and rope each bring a different type of texture to a wall, resulting in a unique statement piece. Hanging this up is sure to spark a lot of positive comments from those who might not be used to seeing these two materials used together in this way.

Tips: You can stain the wood to suit your preferred color and to match other wood décor in the space. You could also paint the wood one solid color or paint a design. For a two-tone look, you can use a different colored cord for the filler or working cords.

Try to avoid splintering on the plywood as you cut and sand. You can use a "20 TPI (teeth per inch) Clean for Wood T-Shank" saw blade for a jigsaw, which is designed specifically for working with plywood and avoiding splintering. I recommend testing your cuts on a scrap piece of wood first. If the wood does splinter in a few spots, you can use a natural-colored wood filler or paint to hide it.

skill level: intermediate

DIMENSIONS
44½ inches (113 cm) wide x 46 inches (117 cm) high

MATERIALS AND TOOLS
Birch plywood 4 feet (1.2 m) wide x 2 feet (61 cm) high x ½ inch (1.3 cm) thick

Pencil

Any thin string approximately 25 inches (63.5 cm) long

Jigsaw

Safety glasses

Fine grit sandpaper

Large sawtooth metal picture hanger pack with small nails

Gorilla Glue (or strong glue of your choice for bonding cotton and wood)

Hammer

About 1,116 feet (340 m) of ³⁄₁₆-inch (5-mm) single-strand cotton string

Staple gun with staples

Screw for hanging

KNOT USED
Vertical Double Half Hitch (page 153)

1. Take your piece of plywood and draw a half circle shape that is 43½ inches (110 cm) wide and 22⅜ inches (57 cm) in height. To get the best shape, tie the string to the pencil and find the center width wise. Hold the end of the string at 22⅜ inches (57 cm) long in the center tightly, and with the pencil tied around the sting, draw a half round shape on the plywood (like a protractor technique). Cut out the shape with the jigsaw. Make sure to wear eye protection and be safe. Sand the edges lightly so that they're smooth.

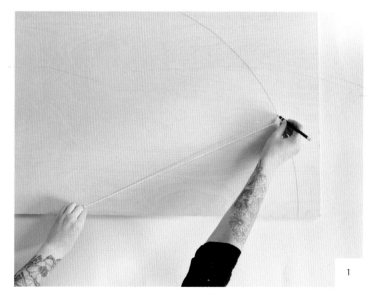

1

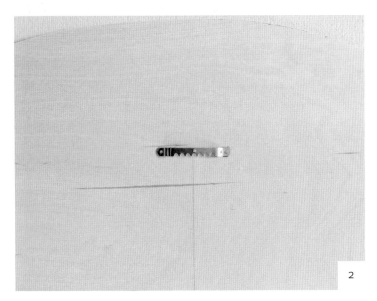

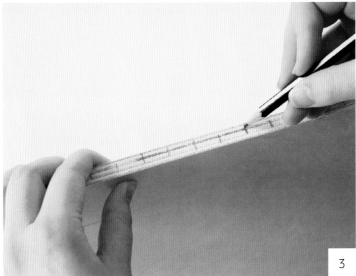

2

3

4

2. To attach the metal picture hanger, on the back of your piece of wood, find the center of the half round shape by measuring across the flat edge, then measure perpendicular from the middle point. Make a mark at 18 inches (46 cm). Line up the center of the metal picture hanger, make sure the metal hanger is level and mark where the holes will be on the wood with a pencil. Add a few drops of Gorilla Glue on the pieces of the metal picture hanger that connect with the wood, line up the metal hanger with your markings and press into place. Once mostly dry, hammer in the small nails that come with the metal picture hanger. Make sure the nails are smaller than the thickness of the wood so that they don't poke through the other side.

3. On the bottom flat edge of the plywood, make a mark with a pencil ½ inch (1.3 cm) in from the end. Then measuring from the ½ inch (1.3 cm) mark, make a mark every ⅝ of an inch (1.6 cm) across the whole edge, which will leave approximately ½ inch (1.3 cm) at the end. This will be where you attach the rope to each marking.

4. Cut 138 pieces of ³⁄₁₆-inch (5-mm) single-strand string, at 4 feet (1.2 m) each. Add a bit of Gorilla Glue on your first marking on the edge of the wood. With two cords, align them so the ends meet, find the middle of both cords and perpendicular to the piece of wood, center both cords with each of your markings/glue on the bottom edge of the wood. While holding the cords in place, use a staple gun to attach the 2 cords. Try to get the staple across both pieces rather than splitting through the string. These cords will be your filler cords. Watch your fingers and make sure your staples are in the middle of the edge, so that they don't come through the front or back of the plywood. Continue this process to each one of the markings with your cords.

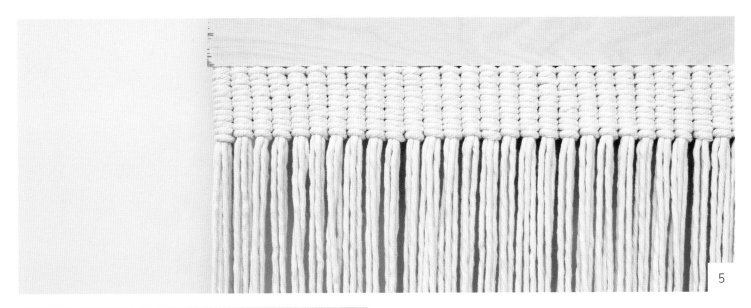

5

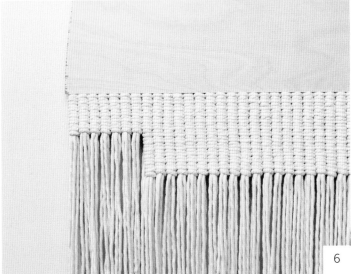

6

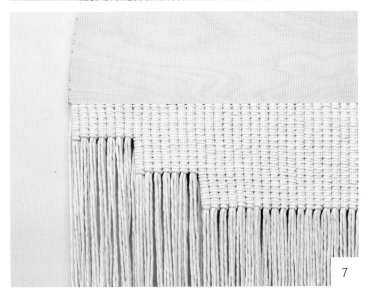

7

5. Cut 6 pieces of ³⁄₁₆-inch (5-mm) single-strand string, at 31 feet (9.5 m) each. These will be your working cords. Position the wall hanging so the rope is hanging off an edge of a flat surface and the wood is sitting on top of a flat surface like a table, so it is easier for you to work. Measuring 2 feet (61 cm) in from the end of a working cord, tie a vertical double half hitch (page 153) around the first 4 filler cords attached to the bottom edge of the wood. Tie it tight to the bottom of the piece of wood. Tie 69 more vertical double half hitches across the bottom with every 4 of the filler cords. Leave the excess working cord to hang with the other cords. You might have to manipulate the cords a bit while you're tying each knot in the first row, so that they sit flush to the wood and evenly side-to-side. With the other 31-foot (9.5-m) working cords, tie 5 more rows of 70 vertical double half hitches with each grouping of 4 filler cords, tight to the row above.

6. Cut 6 pieces of ³⁄₁₆-inch (5-mm) single-strand string, at 24 feet (7.5 m) each. These will be your working cords. Skipping 7 knots from the left, measuring 22 inches (55 cm) in from the end of the working cord, tie 56 vertical double half hitches under and tight to each of the knots above. Leave the excess working cord to hang. With the other 24-foot (7.5-m) working cords, tie 5 more rows of 56 vertical double half hitches with each grouping of filler cords, tight to the knots above.

7. Cut 6 pieces of ³⁄₁₆-inch (5-mm) single-strand string, at 17 feet (5 m) each. These will be your working cords. Skipping 7 knots from the left, measuring 20 inches (51 cm) in from the end of the working cord, tie 42 vertical double half hitches under and tight to each of the knots above and leave the excess working cords to hang. Using the other 17-foot (5-m) working cord, tie 5 more rows of 42 vertical double half hitches with each grouping of filler cords, tight to the knots above.

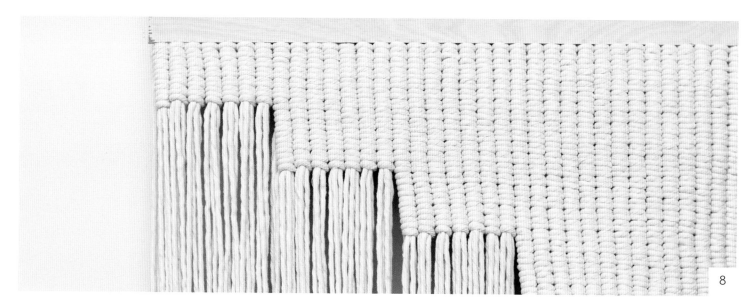

8. Cut 6 pieces of ³/₁₆-inch (5-mm) single-strand string, at 14 feet (4.5 m) each. These will be your working cords. Skipping 7 knots from the left, measuring 18 inches (46 cm) in from the end of the working cord, tie 28 vertical double half hitches under and tight to each of the knots above. Leave the excess working cord to hang. With the other 14-foot (4.5-m) working cords, tie 5 more rows of 28 vertical double half hitches with each grouping of filler cords, tight to the knots above.

9. Cut 6 pieces of ³/₁₆-inch (5-mm) single-strand string, at 8 feet (2.5 m) each. These will be your working cords. Skipping 7 knots from the left, measuring 16 inches (40.5 cm) in from the end of the working cord, tie 14 vertical double half hitches under and tight to each of the knots above and leave the excess working cord to hang. Using the other 8-foot (2.5-m) working cords, tie 5 more rows of 14 vertical double half hitches with each grouping of cords, tight to the knots above.

10. Trim all the cords to 2 feet (61 cm) from the wood or to your preferred height!

hanging tip:

Make sure to hang this piece on a screw that's in a stud or using a drywall anchor that can support its weight. My piece weighed 11¾ pounds (5.5 kg), but to be safe you should always weigh your own finished piece. See page 10 for an easy way to weigh large macramé pieces. Note that if you make any adjustments to the project, it may change the weight.

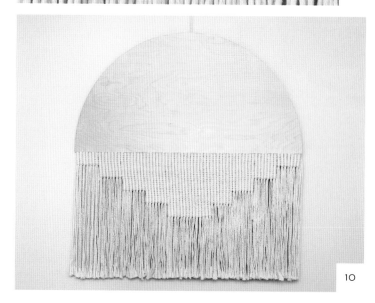

RIVIERE HEADBOARD

I love macramé headboards so much and I know many of you do too, so I figured I would give you two designs to choose from! Or, if you're as crazy about them as I am, you can make them both and put one in a spare room or gift it to a friend. I fell in love with this piece as I was creating it, and I hope you enjoy making it as much as I did. The layers throughout this piece create a depth that I think works really well above a bed. The swooping shapes draw your eye across the design, and the positive and negative space play off each other to create even more depth. I might just switch out the macramé headboard that's been hanging above my bed for the last few years to enjoy this one for a while!

Tip: Try switching out the wood type, staining the wood or using a relatively straight branch to change up the look.

skill level: advanced

DIMENSIONS
69 inches (175 cm) wide (excluding the wood) x 21½ inches (54.5 cm) high

MATERIALS AND TOOLS
About 943 feet (288 m) of ³⁄₁₆-inch (5-mm) single-strand string

1 wood piece 6 feet (1.8 m) long x 1 inch (2.5 cm) wide x ¾ inch (2 cm) thick (I used oak)

Slicker brush

Screws for hanging

KNOTS USED
Lark's Head Knot (page 127)

Continuous Lark's Head Knot (page 150)

Overhand Knot (page 134)

Diamond of Double Half Hitches (connected) (page 156)

Square Knot with Multiple Filler Cords (page 131)

Half Knot Sinnet (left- and right-facing) (page 141)

Gathering Knot (page 138)

Double Half Hitch (page 132)

1. Cut 1 piece of ³⁄₁₆-inch (5-mm) single-strand string, 14 feet (4.5 m) long. Using this piece, leaving a 15-inch (38-cm) tail on the left side of the wood, tie a lark's head knot 1¾ inches (4.5 cm) in from the end of the wood. Now take the other side of the string in your hands, leave a gap of 18 inches (46 cm) on the string and tie a continuous lark's head knot 16¾ inches (42.5 cm) in on the end of the piece of wood. This will create a swooping effect with the string off the wood. Now tie 2 more continuous lark's head knots leaving the same spacing of rope and wood. This creates 4 evenly spaced swooped sections.

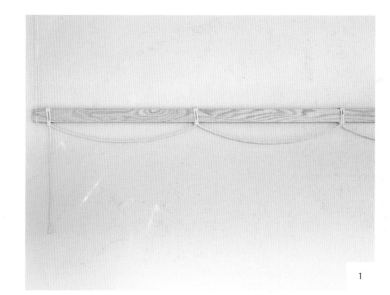

1

2

3

4

2. Tie 1 overhand knot using the tails of rope, directly beneath the lark's head knots on either end of the wood. This secures the two lark's head knots.

3. Cut 168 pieces of ³⁄₁₆-inch (5-mm) single-strand string, each one 2 feet (61 cm) long. Folding each piece in half, using a lark's head knot, attach 42 pieces to each swooped section, totaling 4 sections, which creates a rounded swooping effect for each section. Trim the tails from step 1 to the same length as the 42 pieces.

4. Cut 30 strands of ³⁄₁₆-inch (5-mm) single-strand string, 16 feet (4.9 m) long. Measuring 10¾ inches (27 cm) in the from the left side of the end of the wood, attach 5 pieces of string by folding them in half and attaching with a lark's head knot. Measuring 25¼ inches (64 cm) in from the left side of the end of the piece of wood (within the next section), attach 10 pieces of string the same way. In the next section, measuring 42 inches (107 cm) in from the left side of the end of the wood, attach 10 pieces of string the same way. And in the last section, measuring 59½ inches (151 cm) over from the same side, attach 5 pieces of string in the same way. The two sections on the far right and far left should have 10 cords hanging down, and the two sections in the middle should have 20 cords hanging down.

5

6

7

5. Starting with the 10 cords on the left side of the wood, tie 5 double half hitch diamonds all connected and underneath each other (page 155). Within each diamond tie a square knot with 4 filler cords and 1 working cord on each side (page 157). When tying the diamonds, leave slightly more space between each diamond on the left side— about 1½ to 2 inches (4 to 5 cm)—and tighter spaces between each diamond on the right side— about 1⅛ to 1½ inches (3 to 4 cm). This helps to curve the diamonds toward the right.

6. In the next section to the right, take 10 cords and repeat step 5, but this time leave slightly more space between each diamond on the right side—1½ to 2 inches (4 to 5 cm)—and tighter spaces between each diamond on the left side—1⅛ to 1½ inches (3 to 4 cm). This helps to curve the diamonds toward the left.

7. Bring both strands of diamonds evenly together, leaving a space of 1¼ inch (3 cm) from the bottom of the last diamond, and tie another double half hitch diamond using 10 cords (5 from the right side and 5 from the left side) and the same square knot in the middle with 4 filler cords and 1 working cord on each side.

8. Repeat steps 5 to 7 with the next 2 sections of 10 cords, creating two more Vs of connected diamonds. (Note that there is no photo for this step.)

9

10

11

9. Under the connected V of diamonds on the left side, use the 4 cords at the bottom to tie a left-facing half knot sinnet with a total of 9 half knots in each sinnet. It will twist toward the right. Tie a right-facing half knot sinnet with the bottom 4 cords on the far right connected V of diamonds. It will twist to the left. This way both outer sections are twisting toward the middle.

10. With the middle 4 cords from the bottom of the middle connected V of diamonds, tie a right-facing half knot sinnet with a total of 12 half knots.

11. Cut 3 pieces of ³⁄₁₆-inch (5-mm) single-stand string, 21 inches (53 cm) long. Using these cords, tie a total of 3 gathering knots ¾ inch (2 cm) long at the base of each half knot sinnet.

12

13

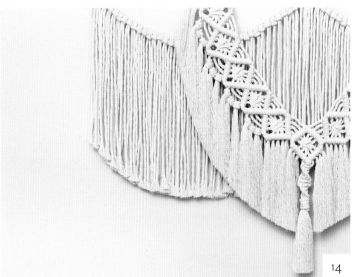

14

12. Cut 80 pieces of ³⁄₁₆-inch (5-mm) single-strand string, each 16 inches (40.5 cm) long. Fold each of these cords in half, and using a lark's head knot, attach each cord to the 3-inch (7.5-cm) space between the diamonds. The space closest to the wood on the far right and far left sides will only have 2 pieces attached, and the space closest to the wood on the middle connected V of diamonds will only have 1 piece attached on each side. This is so the fringe is not too full in the middle and because the spaces on the far ends will not fit 3 pieces.

13. Trim the 16 pieces of string hanging from the bottom of the Vs of double half hitch diamonds to roughly the same lengths of the pieces of string you just attached in the previous step. Then fully brush out the string attached to the connected Vs of double half hitch, the pieces you just cut, and the tassels underneath the gathering knots around the half knot sinnets. Use the slicker brush technique (page 159).

14. Trim the fringe you just brushed out to the shape shown in the photos or your desired shape. I cut the top of my fringe to approximately 5 inches (13 cm) and 6 inches (15 cm) at the bottom. Be mindful and avoid accidentally cutting the layer hanging behind it. To get a precise looking shape, you will need to brush and trim off little by little continually until you are happy with the result. Trim the 3 tassels to approximately 21¾ inches (55 cm) when measuring from the top of the wood, a little longer than the rest of your fringe.

15. Tidy up the back layer of string by slightly trimming and making sure all pieces are ending at an even length. You are done!

To hang the headboard, see page 20 and follow the same advice. My piece weighed 3 pounds (1.5 kg), but to be safe you should always weigh your own finished piece. See page 10 for an easy way to weigh large macramé pieces. Note that if you make any adjustments to the project, it may change the weight.

15

LEDA WALL HANGING

This is one of my favorite styles of macramé to create. Some of my earliest designs looked a lot like this piece, and I continue to work with this style because it fits so many uses. This statement wall hanging can work just about anywhere; over a bed or couch, above a sideboard, in a business setting or even as a backdrop for an event. The options are endless for this piece! Its dense, varying patterns keep your eye excited as it moves across the piece discovering balance along the way through the changing knots.

Tips: The straighter you can keep the rows, the better the piece will look. Take your time tying each knot at the right height and even with the surrounding knots. Keep in mind that this level of precision takes time and practice, so go easy on yourself if it looks a bit wobbly at first—so was mine!

Pull tight horizontally on your tied double half hitches throughout a row, while holding the filler cord to keep your knots even throughout the pattern. If you want to change the width of this wall hanging, work in groups of 10 cords.

skill level: advanced

DIMENSIONS
45¾ inches (116 cm) wide (excluding dowel) x 43 inches (109 cm) high

MATERIALS AND TOOLS
About 1,359 feet (414.2 m) of ³⁄₁₆-inch (5-mm) three-strand rope

1 wood dowel 56 inches (142 cm) long

Large-eye needle

Screws for hanging

KNOTS USED
Lark's Head Knot (page 127)

Double Half Hitch (page 132)

Alternating Square Knot (Increasing & Diagonal rows) (page 143)

Single and Double Arrow Double Half Hitch (page 157)

Square Knot Sinnet (page 140)

Square Knot (page 130)

Horizontal & Diagonal Double Half Hitch (page 151)

Square Knot with Multiple Filler Cords (page 131)

1. Cut 60 pieces of ³⁄₁₆-inch (5-mm) three-strand rope, 22 feet (6.7 m) long. Fold each cord in half and attach and center on the dowel using a lark's head knot. Make sure the cords are evenly spaced and not squished together. This will leave 5½ inches (14 cm) of blank space on the dowel on either side.

Then cut 7 pieces of ³⁄₁₆-inch (5-mm) three-strand rope, each 54½ inches (138.5 cm) long, and set aside. Lastly cut 1 piece of ³⁄₁₆-inch (5-mm) three-strand rope, 78½ inches (199.5 cm) long, and set aside.

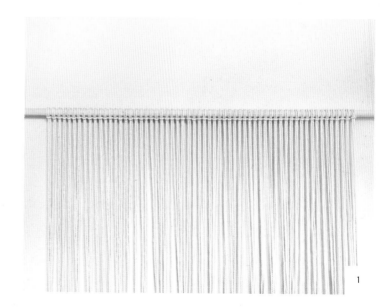

1

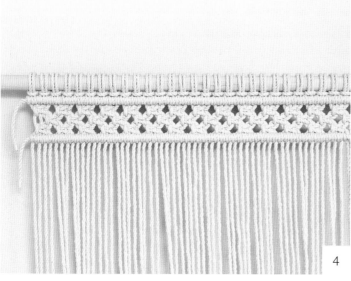

2. Using one of the 54½-inch (138.5-cm) pieces as a filler cord, leave a 5-inch (13-cm) tail at the beginning of the row, and tie 120 double half hitches with each of the cords. This will leave a short tail on the right side of the wall hanging as well. These tails will later be sewn into the back of the wall hanging.

3. Tie 3 rows of alternating square knots with every cord, tight to the row above and leaving no space between each row of square knots.

4. Using one more of the 54½-inch (138.5-cm) pieces as a filler cord, repeat step 2, again leaving a 5-inch (13-cm) tail at the beginning of the row, and tying 120 double half hitches with each of the cords. This will leave a short tail on the right side of the wall hanging as well.

5. Tight to the row above, tie a row of 12 double half hitch arrows (page 157) that point down, using a total of 10 cords each. Tie another double half hitch arrow directly underneath the one you just tied, creating 12 double arrows.

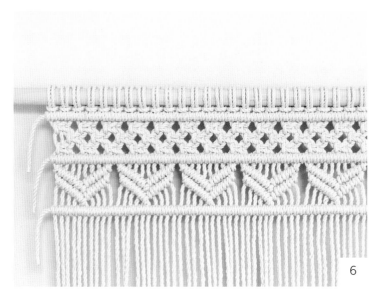

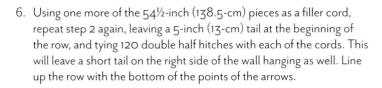

6

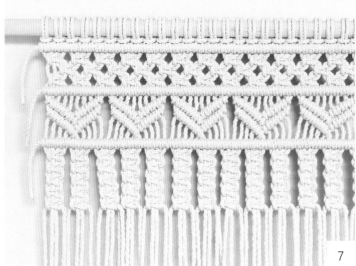

7

6. Using one more of the 54½-inch (138.5-cm) pieces as a filler cord, repeat step 2 again, leaving a 5-inch (13-cm) tail at the beginning of the row, and tying 120 double half hitches with each of the cords. This will leave a short tail on the right side of the wall hanging as well. Line up the row with the bottom of the points of the arrows.

7. Tight to the row above, tie 30 square knot sinnets, each consisting of 5 square knots in each sinnet. Each square knot sinnet should be about 3⅝ inches (9 cm) long.

8. Using one more of the 54½-inch (138.5-cm) pieces as a filler cord, repeat step 2 again, leaving a 5-inch (13-cm) tail at the beginning of the row, and tying 120 double half hitches with each of the cords. This will leave a short tail on the right side of the wall hanging as well.

9. Counting 6 cords in from the left, tie 2 square knots side by side. Then tie one alternating square knot in the middle, on the next row below the square knots you just tied, leaving no space between the rows. Counting 12 cords to the right, tie the same grouping of 3 square knots you just tied. Repeat this 4 more times.

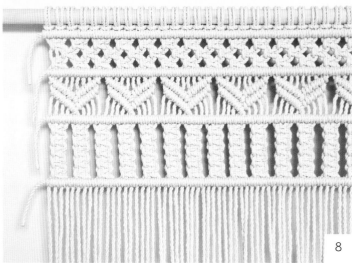

8

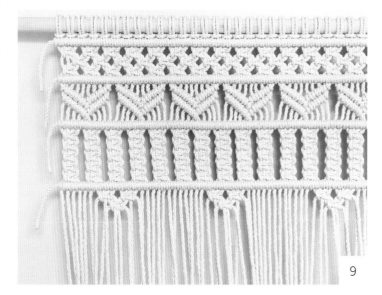

9

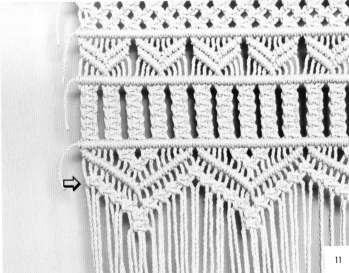

10. On the left of the wall hanging, counting 6 cords to the right of the first set of square knots, angle the sixth cord down and to the left at a 35- to 40-degree angle. This will become a filler cord. Tie 9 diagonal double half hitches around the filler cord. With the very first cord on the left of the wall hanging, hold it at a 35- to 40-degree angle down and to the right, and tie 10 diagonal double half hitches around it. The tenth double half hitch will join the two rows together. Repeat these same steps around each of the 5 remaining sets of 3 square knots. This will create a total of 6 V shapes.

11. Starting on the left side of the wall hanging, 1 inch (2.5 cm) below the row of double half hitches, tie a row of 4 alternating square knots, angling down and to the right. Starting where the first indicator is, measuring 1 inch (2.5 cm) below the double half hitches, tie a row of 5 alternating square knots, angling down and to the left. Join both rows of alternating square knots together by tying a square knot sinnet consisting of 2 square knots. Repeat this same pattern of alternating square knots across the wall hanging a total of 5 more times.

12. In the middle of the square knot sinnets you just tied, count 12 cords out in both directions from the very middle, leaving 2 cords on either side. Tie a large square knot with 10 filler cords and 1 working cord on both sides. Don't pull the large square knot so tight that it bunches all the filler cords together; instead, pull it just tight enough that it keeps them next to each other, side by side. Repeat this a total of 5 times between each of the square knot sinnets. On the far left and right side of the wall hanging, count 6 cords from the outer edge, and tie a large square knot with 4 filler cords, leaving the two cords next to the square knot sinnet alone.

13

13. Starting on the left side of the wall hanging underneath the square knot sinnets you previously tied, tie a row of 4 alternating square knots angling down and to the left. *Back under the square knot sinnet, tie a row of 4 alternating square knots angling down and to the right. Try to match the same angles as the rows of alternating square knots you just tied above. On the next square knot sinnet to the right, tie a row of 5 alternating square knots angling down and to the left. The fifth square knot will join the two rows together.* Repeat between the **5 more times. Finish the last section by tying a row of 4 alternating square knots angling down and to the right.

14

14. Under the last row of square knots, in the middle of each of the upside-down Vs, working in groups of 20 cords, with the tenth and eleventh cords in the middle, tie a row of 10 double half hitches, 1 inch (2.5 cm) below the square knots, angling down and to the right. Under the first double half hitch, using the first working cord as a filler cord for your next row, tie 9 double half hitches, 1 inch (2.5 cm) below the row above. Repeat this 5 more times across the wall hanging.

15. Under each of the inverted double half hitch Vs, in the middle (under the point), tie a square knot ¾ inch (2 cm) below the point of the double half hitches. Tie two increasing alternating square knots below the last knot you just tied. Do this 5 more times under each of the inverted Vs.

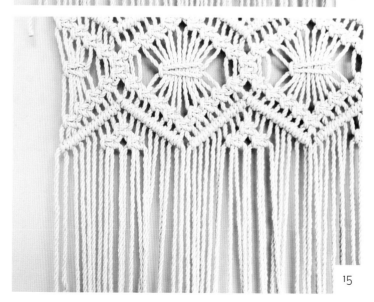

15

16

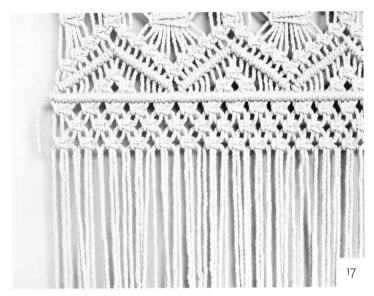

17

18

16. Using one more of the 54½-inch (138.5-cm) pieces as a filler cord, repeat step 2 again, leaving a 5-inch (13-cm) tail at the beginning of the row and tying 120 double half hitches with each of the cords. This will leave a short tail on the right side of the wall hanging as well. Keep the row straight and tight to the square knots you just tied and the lower double half hitches from the inverted Vs in the previous row.

17. Tie 3 rows of alternating square knots. Tie the first row of square knots tight to the row of double half hitches above, and leave a ¾-inch (2-cm) gap between the next 2 rows of alternating square knots.

18. Using one more of the 54½-inch (138.5-cm) pieces as a filler cord, repeat step 2 again, leaving a 5-inch (13-cm) tail at the beginning of the row and tying 120 double half hitches with each of the cords tight to the row above. This will leave a short tail on the right side of the wall hanging.

19. Tight to the row above, tie a row of 12 double half hitch arrows that point up, using a total of 10 cords each. Tie another arrow directly underneath the ones you just tied, creating 12 double half hitch double arrows.

19

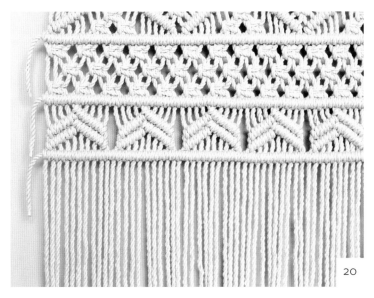

20

21

20. Using the last of the 54½-inch (138.5-cm) pieces as a filler cord, one last time repeat step 2, leaving a 5-inch (13-cm) tail at the beginning of the row, and tying 120 double half hitches with each of the cords tight to the base of the arrows from the row above. This will leave a short tail on the right side of the wall hanging.

21. Leaving a gap that is 1¾ inches (4.5 cm), using the 78½-inch (199-cm) piece as a filler cord and leaving a 12-inch (30.5-cm) tail at the beginning of the row, tie 120 double half hitches with each of the cords. This will leave an approximate 12-inch (30.5-cm) tail on the right side of the wall hanging as well. These tails become a part of the fringe.

22. Unravel all of the tails from the filler cords. Turn the wall hanging around so you are looking at the back. Using a large-eye needle, sew each unraveled strand into the back of the third double half hitch from the end.

23. Cut all of the cords to 11 inches (27.9 cm) long or your desired length, measuring from the last row. Then unravel all of the cords using the fringe technique (page 159). Do a final trim to clean up the fringe and you're finished!

Hang with the same technique from page 20. My piece weighed 8 pounds (3.5 kg), but to be safe you should always weigh your own finished piece. See page 10 for an easy way to weigh large macramé pieces. Note that if you make any adjustments to the project, it may change the weight.

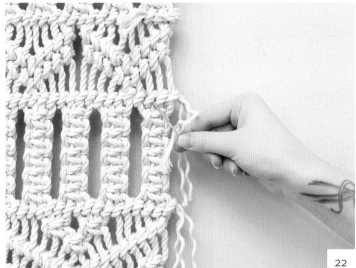

22

23

plant hangers & HOME DÉCOR

Plants and macramé were truly meant for one another. Each one perfectly complements the other's design and beauty, so it's no surprise that many people's first experience with macramé is through plant hangers. In fact, the first piece of macramé that I ever created was a plant hanger! Like plants, macramé plant hangers can come in all different types and sizes. Since this book is focused on large-scale art pieces, I wanted to design plant hangers and home décor that would make people stop and take a second look, which will most definitely happen because one plant hanger is almost 6 feet (1.8 m) tall (page 55) and the other holds up to five plants (page 47)!

My goal when using macramé for home décor is to create unique designs that have the power to transform the space they're in. The rug (page 65) and hanging table (page 43) in this chapter accomplish that and also happen to be some of my favorite projects in the whole book! They each come with their own unique set of challenges to overcome and might not be the best projects to start if you're in the mood to finish something quickly, but if you give yourself enough time I know you'll be able to create these incredible pieces for yourself and will love the outcome.

CURRENT HANGING SIDE TABLE

I fell in love with this side table as soon as I finished making it! I set out to create something unique that also serves a purpose, and I think this project embodies that perfectly. It has a modern and elegant design yet is also eclectic and adds some fun to the room! You can style it with some books, a plant and some of your favorite small pieces of décor. Hang it next to a bed, a couch, a chair, a desk or wherever you'd like. The compact design makes a statement wherever it is!

This may be the cat lady in me talking, but you can also place a round cushion on top of the wood (see below) and use it as a cute cat bed! Just make sure it's hung securely to handle the weight and keep your kitties safe.

Tip: Seal the wood with a stain of your choice to keep it looking fresh longer. I used a clear stain.

skill level: intermediate

DIMENSIONS
16½ inches (42 cm) in diameter x 81 inches (206 cm) tall (with wood in place)

MATERIALS AND TOOLS
About 290 feet (88.4 m) of ³⁄₁₆-inch (5-mm) braided rope

2-inch (5-cm) wood ring

6-inch (15-cm) bamboo embroidery hoop (using the inner hoop only)

Something round and 16 inches (40.5 cm) in diameter to trace or a 10-inch (25.5-cm) piece of string

Pencil

16-inch (40.5-cm)-diameter round piece of plywood (or a round glass tabletop)

Jigsaw

Safety glasses

Fine grit sandpaper

Wood stain (optional)

Ceiling or wall hook for hanging

KNOTS USED
Gathering Knot (page 138)

Double Half Hitch (page 132)

Double Half Hitch Around a Ring or Dowel (page 151)

Overhand Knot (page 134)

Horizontal Double Half Hitch (page 151)

1. Cut 9 pieces of ³⁄₁₆-inch (5-mm) braided rope, each 28 feet (8.5 m) long. Fold each cord in half and attach through the 2-inch (5-cm) wood ring, so there are 14 feet (4.3 m) of rope hanging down on either side. Some of the cords are hidden underneath each other, so it may look like fewer cords in the photo. Cut 1 piece of ³⁄₁₆-inch (5-mm) braided rope, 40 inches (101.6 cm) long. Fold it at 3½ inches (9 cm) from one end and tie a 1½-inch (4-cm)-long gathering knot around all of the cords tight to the wood ring.

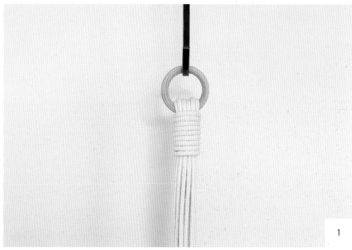

2

3

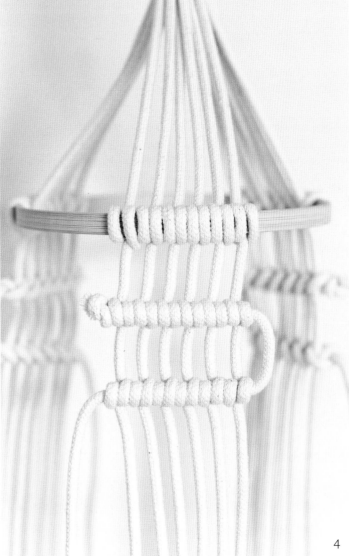

4

2. Divide the cords evenly into 3 sections, with 6 cords in each section. In one section, measuring 5 inches (13 cm) down from the base of the gathering knot, tie 6 double half hitches around the inner embroidery hoop (page 151). Make sure to keep the embroidery hoop level from all angles before you finish the double half hitches. Measure 3¼ inches (8 cm) over on the embroidery hoop from the last double half hitch you tied, and tie another 6 double half hitches with the next section of cords. Repeat this one more time with the last section of cords. The sections of cords should be evenly spaced around the hoop.

3. Cut 3 pieces of ³⁄₁₆-inch (5-mm) braided rope, 10 feet (3 m) long. These cords will be used as continuous filler cords throughout the full length of the piece. *Tie an overhand knot at the very end of one of the 10-foot (3-m) cords. Using this cord as the filler cord and placing the overhand knot you just tied on the left of one of the three sections, measuring ¾ inch (2 cm) down, tie 6 horizontal double half hitches across the section (working left to right). Slightly pull on all of the double half hitches by holding the filler cord, so they get slightly squished tight together.* Repeat between the * * on the other 2 sections with the other 2 pieces of 10-foot (3-m) rope.

4. Now working right to left, measuring 1³⁄₈ inches (3.5 cm) down on the filler cord from the last double half hitch from the last row, and ¾ inch (2 cm) down on the working cord from the same knot, tie a row of 6 horizontal double half hitches around the same filler cord. This creates a loop on the right connecting both rows of double half hitches. Slightly pull on all of the double half hitches by holding the filler cord, so they get slightly squished tight together, but not so much that they slide out of place. Repeat this on the other two sections.

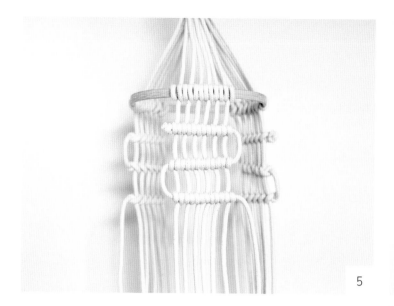

5

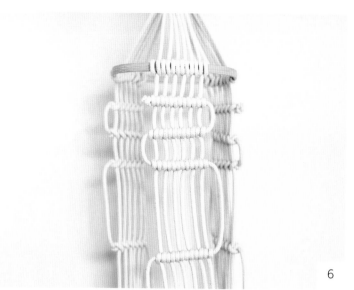

6

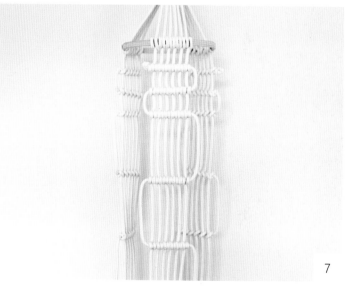

7

5. Working left to right, measuring 1⅜ inches (3.5 cm) down on the filler cord from the last double half hitch from the last row, and ¾ inch (2 cm) down on the working cord from the same knot, tie a row of 6 horizontal double half hitches around the same filler cord. This creates a loop on the left connecting both rows of double half hitches. Slightly pull on all of the double half hitches by holding the filler cord, so they get slightly squished tight together, but not so much that they slide out of place. Repeat this on the other two sections.

6. Working right to left, measuring 4 inches (10 cm) down on the filler cord from the last double half hitch from the last row, and 3⅜ inches (8.5 cm) down on the working cord from the same knot, tie a row of 6 horizontal double half hitches around the same filler cord. This creates a larger loop on the right connecting both rows of double half hitches. Slightly pull on all of the double half hitches by holding the filler cord, so they get slightly squished tight together. Repeat this on the other two sections.

7. Working left to right, measuring 4 inches (10 cm) down on the filler cord from the last double half hitch from the last row, and 3⅜ inches (8.5 cm) down on the working cord from the same knot, tie a row of 6 horizontal double half hitches around the same filler cord. This creates a larger loop on the left connecting both rows of double half hitches. Slightly pull on all of the double half hitches by holding the filler cord, so they get slightly squished tight together. Repeat this on the other two sections.

8. In each of the 3 sections, repeat steps 4 to 7 four times.

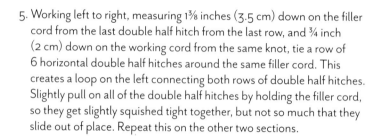

8

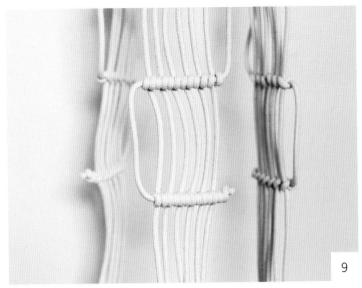

9

10

11

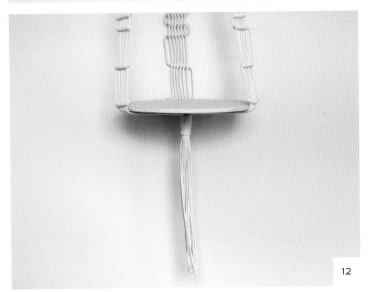

12

9. In each of the 3 sections, tie an overhand knot tight next to the last double half hitch and cut the excess rope close to the knot.

10. Cut 1 piece of ³⁄₁₆-inch (5-mm) braided rope, 50 inches (127 cm) long. Measuring 8¼ inches (21 cm) down from the last row of knots in each of the sections, from one end of the 50-inch (127-cm) rope, fold at 4 inches (10 cm) and tie a 2-inch (5-cm) wide gathering knot around all of the cords. Make sure this knot is tied tightly and securely, as it will be supporting the weight of the table on top of it.

11. Cut all of the cords 16 inches (40.5 cm) from the bottom of the gathering knot.

12. Draw a 16-inch (40.5-cm) circle on the plywood by tracing something of a similar size or by tying a 10-inch (25.5-cm) piece of string to a pencil so that it's 8 inches (20 cm) in length (similar to using a protractor). Wearing safety glasses, cut out the circle with a jigsaw. Give the edges of the circle a light sanding. Place your round 16-inch (40.5-cm)-diameter piece of plywood or glass into the middle of the 3 sections. Make sure to evenly space the 3 sections of macramé around the circle to properly support the table. Keep the wood natural or seal with your preferred stain to protect the wood from daily use.

hanging tips:

Make sure to screw a ceiling hook or wall hook into a stud or a drywall anchor that will support the weight of whatever you place on top of the table. Note that if you make any adjustments to the project, it may change the weight.

Use another piece of rope to hang it at the right height from the ceiling or use an outdoor extra-long plant hook to hang it at the appropriate height off the wall.

RAVANA PLANT HANGER

Anyone who knows me even a little bit knows that I absolutely love plants, so I am down for any excuse to have multiple plants hanging around the house! I created this asymmetrical multi-plant hanger with a repeating pattern so that it would showcase the plants it's holding while still attracting some attention with the subtle movement and repetition throughout the piece. As a cross between a macramé wall hanging and plant hanger, I love this piece as a focal point over a sideboard, couch or bed.

Any trailing plant looks great in this plant hanger. I choose my favorite, low-maintenance plant to use in this plant hanger: the pothos! Some trailing plants you could try are heart-shaped philodendrons, ivies, hoyas or spider plants! The beauty of this macramé plant hanger is that the choice is all yours!

Tips: I used 5 terracotta pots that are all 3 inches (7.5 cm) in diameter, which fit this design perfectly. If you would like to use slightly larger pots, when you get to steps 17 and 18, make the openings slightly larger to accommodate the pot size you would like! I wouldn't recommend using pots larger than 5 inches (13 cm) because of how the knots are tied. Larger pots could slip through.

The pots I used have drainage holes, so I take the pots out of the hanger to water the plants.

skill level: advanced

DIMENSIONS
40 inches (101.5 cm) wide (excluding the wood) x 33½ inches (85 cm) high

MATERIALS AND TOOLS
About 810 feet (247 m) of ³⁄₁₆-inch (5-mm) three-strand rope

1 wood piece 4 feet (1.2 m) long x ½ inch (1.3 cm) thick x 1 inch (2.5 cm) wide (I used oak)

Slicker brush

Screws for hanging

KNOTS USED
Lark's Head Knot (page 127)

Half Knot Sinnet (left- and right-facing) (page 141)

Alternating Square Knot (page 143)

Square Knot (page 130)

Gathering Knot (page 138)

1. Cut 16 pieces of ³⁄₁₆-inch (5-mm) three-strand rope, each 10 feet (3 m) long. Cut 40 pieces of ³⁄₁₆-inch (5-mm) three-strand rope, each 16 feet (5 m) long. Cut 5 pieces of ³⁄₁₆-inch (5-mm) three-strand rope, each 2 feet (61 cm) long and set aside for later. Fold 8 pieces of the 10-foot (3-m) cords in half and attach to the left side of the piece of wood with a lark's head knot. Attach all 40 pieces of the 16-foot (5-m) cords to the right of the previously attached cords the same way. Then attach the last 8 pieces of 10-foot (3-m) cords to the right of the previously attached strands with a lark's head knot. Make sure to center all 56 strands on the piece of wood.

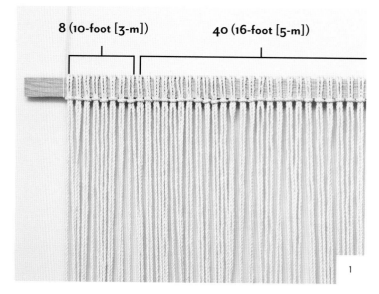

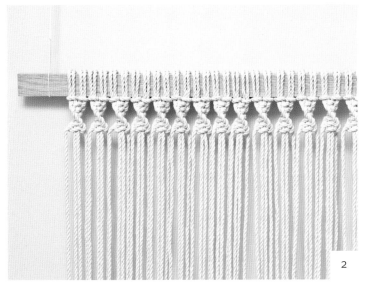

2

3

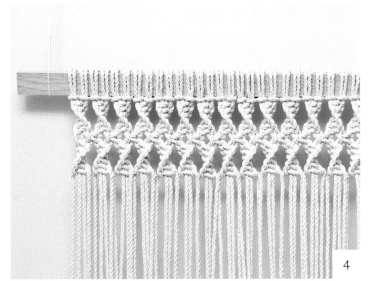

4

2. Tie 28 left-facing half knot sinnets across all 56 strands of rope, with each sinnet having 5 half knots in it. Make sure to tie them tight to the piece of wood. The sinnets should spiral to the right. Note that in the photo, I've only showed part of the sinnets, not the whole row, so you can see the detail close up.

3. Tie 27 alternating square knots across the whole row, tight to the row above.

4. Alternating cords, tie another set of 28 half knot sinnets, this time using right-facing half knots, across all 56 strands of rope, tight to the square knots above. Again, each sinnet should have 5 half knots in it. The sinnets should now spiral to the left.

5. Tie 27 alternating square knots across the whole row, tight to the row above.

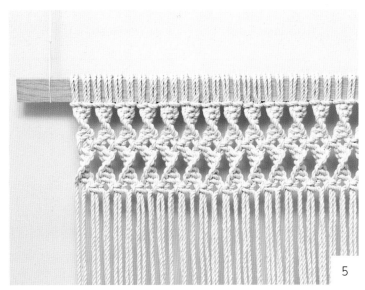

5

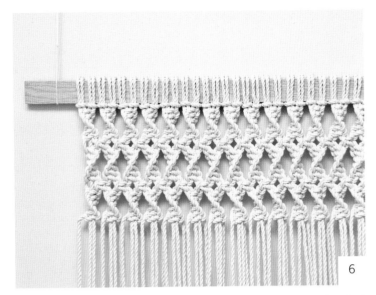

6

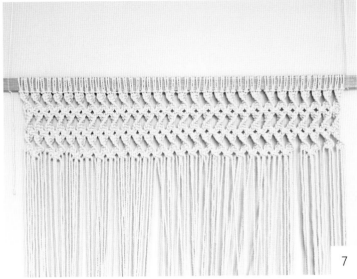

7

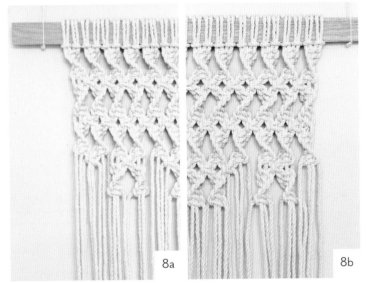

8a   8b

6. Alternating cords, tie 5 left-facing half knots, creating a half knot sinnet made up of 5 knots each, across all 56 strands, tight to the square knots above. These sinnets now spiral to the right.

7. Working left to right, tie 1 alternating square knot tight to the knots above, then skip 4 cords, then tie 1 alternating square knot tight to the knots above. Skip another 4 cords and tie 20 alternating square knots tight to the knots above. Skip 4 cords, then tie 1 alternating square knot.

8. Working left to right, skip 8 cords, then tie 2 right-facing half knot sinnets consisting of 5 half knots in each. Skip the next 4 cords, tie 19 right-facing half knot sinnets consisting of 5 half knots in each. Skip over the next 4 cords, and tie 2 right-facing half knot sinnets consisting of 5 half knots in each.

9. Working left to right, starting where the arrow is (skipping the first 18 cords), tie 19 alternating square knots tight to the knots above.

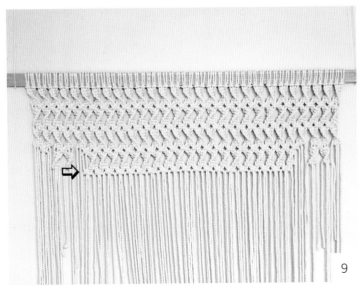

9

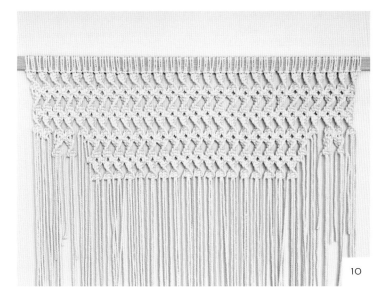
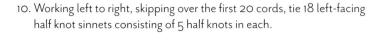

10

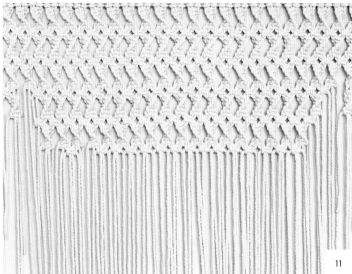

11

10. Working left to right, skipping over the first 20 cords, tie 18 left-facing half knot sinnets consisting of 5 half knots in each.

11. Working left to right, skipping over the first 26 cords, tie 1 alternating square knot tight to the knots above. Skip over the next 4 cords, and tie 14 alternating square knots tight to the knots above.

12. Working left to right, skipping over the first 24 cords, tie 2 right-facing half knot sinnets consisting of 5 half knots in each. Skip over the next 4 cords, and tie 13 right-facing half knot sinnets consisting of 5 half knots each.

13. Working left to right, skipping over the first 38 cords, tie 8 alternating square knots tight to the knots above them. Skip over the next 8 cords and tie 1 alternating square knot tight to the row above.

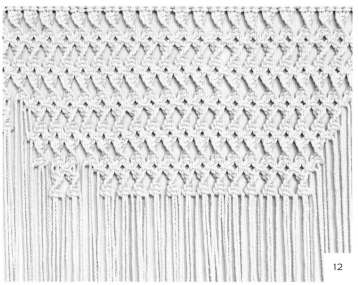

12

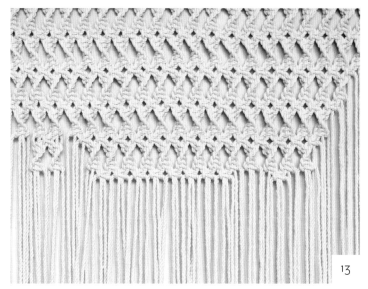

13

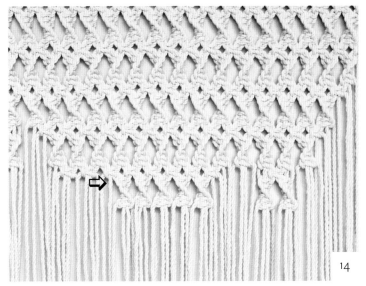

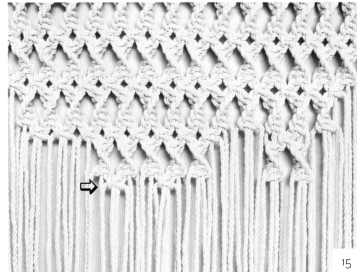

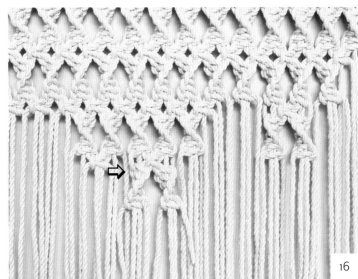

14. Working left to right, skipping over the first 48 cords (starting where the arrow is), tie 5 left-facing half knot sinnets, each consisting of 5 half knots, tight to the row above. Skip the next 8 cords and tie 2 more left-facing half knot sinnets consisting of 5 half knots in each, tight to the row above.

15. Working left to right, skipping over the first 50 cords (starting where the arrow is), tie 1 alternating square knot tight to the row above. Skip 4 cords and tie another alternating square knot tight to the row above.

16. Working left to right, skipping over the first 56 cords (starting where the arrow is), tie 2 right-facing half knot sinnets consisting of 5 half knots in each, tight to the row above. It is OK if some of your cords are getting short; they will hide in the fringe.

17. Using the 2 adjacent cords (marked in yellow) on either side of where the plant will sit, bring both cords together and in front of the other knots, so you now have 4 cords to tie a square knot, 3 inches (7.5 cm) down on these cords from the knots above. Do this a total of 5 times in each of the marked spots.

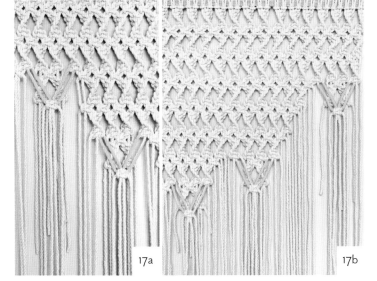

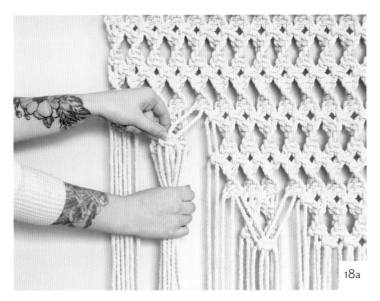

18a

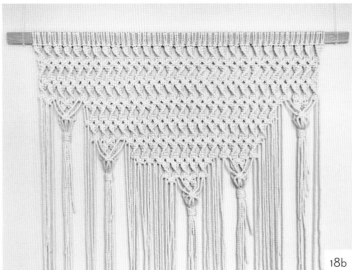

18b

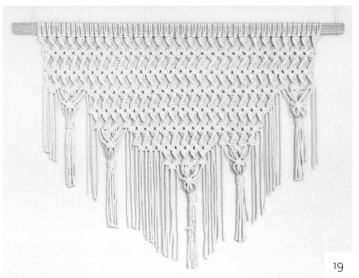

19

18a. In those same spots, with a loose fist, group the 8 cords from the 2 half knot sinnets behind the square knot you just tied, and the 4 cords from the square knot you just tied (totaling 12 cords). Pull upwards on the square knot just a little, giving these 4 cords more slack.

18b. Take one of the 2-foot (61-cm) cords that were set aside and tie a ¾-inch (2-cm)-wide gathering knot around all 12 cords so it is approximately 2 inches (5 cm) down from the square knot, and 1½ inches (4 cm) down from the half knot sinnets. These two different rope lengths create a small pocket for your pot to sit in. Repeat this for each of the spots shown in step 17, totaling 5 gathering knots.

Note: As mentioned in the tip on page 47, if you are using slightly larger pots, you would make larger openings for them in step 18 by pulling up on the square knot a little more. So your 2 inches (5 cm) and 1½ inches (4 cm) in this step would be a little larger. As mentioned, don't use pots too much larger, since the design of this pocket isn't meant to hold large pots.

19. Trim the cords to your desired length following the shape of the knots. I trimmed the cords between 8 and 12 inches (20 and 30 cm) to get this asymmetric shape.

20. Unravel each of the cords and then unravel each of those strands to get a fuller look (page 158). I slightly brushed out just the ends with a slicker brush to make it even thicker (page 159). Clean up the edges with a final trim. Find your favorite plants and pots, hang and enjoy your hard work!

Plant hangers can get heavy, especially when you add in the pots, soil and plants. For this project I recommend weighing your finished piece with the plants. See page 10 for an easy way to weigh large macramé pieces.

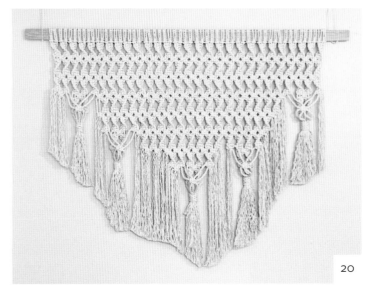

20

JUNIPER PLANT HANGER

It's safe to say that macramé and plants are a match made in heaven. My house is full of them, and I wouldn't have it any other way! This tall plant hanger will look amazing in any corner of a room, or even hanging from a curtain rod! It works well on its own or can be paired with smaller plant hangers around it to create a hanging garden that breathes life into a space. The fun continues even after you finish making this project, because that's when you get to choose the types of plants you'd like to hang! I prefer hanging plants that will trail down as they grow like a pothos, heart-leafed philodendron, spider plants and ivy.

Tip: Do your best to keep the hoops level from every angle. It can be easy to keep it level from one vantage point, but keep checking from other angles as you work. I suggest you use 6- to 8-inch (15- to 20-cm)-size pots. If you use pots that are smaller than that, they won't push the rope out, which I think looks best.

skill level: advanced

DIMENSIONS
6 inches (15 cm) wide x 67 inches (170 cm) tall (without plants in it)

MATERIALS AND TOOLS
About 749 feet (228 m) of ⁵⁄₆₄-inch (2-mm) single-strand string

1 (2½-inch [6.5-cm]-diameter) metal ring

3 (5-inch [13-cm]-diameter) metal rings

Fabric glue (optional) (I suggest Aleene's Original Tacky Glue since it's all-purpose and nontoxic)

Slicker brush

Curtain rod or ceiling hook for hanging

KNOTS USED
Gathering Knot (page 138)

Square Knot (page 130)

Cluster of 4 Square Knots (page 148)

Double Half Hitch (page 132)

Double Half Hitch Around a Ring or Dowel (page 151)

Alternating Square Knot (page 143)

Wrapping a Ring in Rope (page 152)

Increasing Alternating Square Knot (page 146)

Decreasing Alternating Square Knot (page 145)

Row of Diagonal Alternating Square Knots (page 147)

Diamond of Double Half Hitches (page 156)

Macadamia Knot (page 137)

Continuous Lark's Head Knot (page 150)

Reef Knot (page 135)

1. Cut 18 pieces of ⁵⁄₆₄-inch (2-mm) single-strand string, each 24 feet (7.5 m) long. Group the cords so the ends align. Fold the grouped cords in half to find the center. Cut one piece of ⁵⁄₆₄-inch (2-mm) single-strand string, 7 feet (2.1 m) long. Fold the 7-foot (2.1-m) cord 7 inches (17.5 cm) in from one end and tie a 5-inch (13-cm)-wide gathering knot in the middle and around all 18 of the 24-foot (7.5-m) cords.

1

2

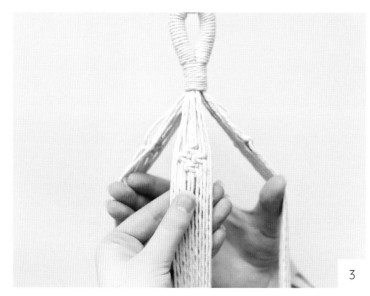

3

4

2. Cut 1 piece of 5/64-inch (2-mm) single-strand string, 2½ feet (76 cm) long. Fold the now gathered ropes in half again and line up the beginning and end of the gathering knot. Fold the 2½-foot (76-cm) cord, 1½ inches (4 cm) in from one end, and tie a ⅞-inch (2-cm)-wide gathering knot so it is right below the now looped gathering knot.

3. Group all of the cords into 3 groups of 12. I found it easier to bundle each of the cords before working with them (page 158) but do whatever is easiest for you.

   In each of the 3 sections, measuring 1¾ inches (4.5 cm) down, tie a cluster of 4 square knots (page 148) in the middle of the 12 cords (this leaves 2 cords on either side of the cluster, in each section).

4. Using the 2½-inch (6.5-cm) metal ring, measuring 1¾ inches (4.5 cm) down from the last square knot, tie 1 double half hitch around the hoop (page 151) with each of the 36 cords. This will completely cover the ring. If you start running out of room on the ring and still have more double half hitches to tie, push the knots on the ring tighter together to give you more room.

5. Directly under the ring you just tied onto, tie 9 square knots with every 4 cords. Then, leaving a ½-inch (1.3-cm) space between each row, tie 4 rows of alternating square knots.

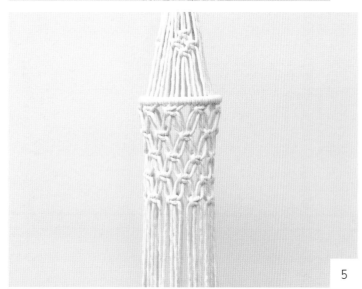

5

6. Cut 3 pieces of ⁵⁄₆₄-inch (2-mm) single-strand string at 8 feet (2.5 m) long. Using a 5-inch (13-cm) ring and one of the 8-foot (2.5-m) strands, tie 2 double half hitches with the end of the 8-foot (2.5-m) string around the ring. Then start wrapping the ring tightly until you are ⅛ inch (3 mm) from the 2 double half hitches you tied. To secure the wrapping, tie 2 more double half hitches around the ring (see Wrapping a Ring in Rope on page 152). Pull on both ends to make sure your knots are tight, then cut both ends to ⅛ inch (3 mm) long. If you are worried your knots won't stay tight, you can add a few very small drops of glue to each of the 4 double half hitches you tied. Wrap the two other 5-inch (13-cm) rings the same way and set aside for later.

7. Holding the wrapped ring directly under the last row of square knots, place the filler cords from the square knots on the inside of the hoop and the working cords on the outside. Tie another 9 square knots directly under the previous square knots, keeping each knot 1½ inches (4 cm) apart from each other so they are evenly spaced around the ring. This will secure the ring in place, so make sure you are tying the square knots tight. Try to hide the ends of the double half hitches from the wrapped ring under one of the knotted sections.

8. Section all of the cords into 3 groups of 12. With the middle 4 cords in each section, tie 1 square knot 1½ inches (4 cm) down from the ring. In each section, tie 2 rows of increasing alternating square knots with ¼ inch (6 mm) of space between each row.

9

10

11

9. In each of the 3 sections, tie 20 rows of alternating square knots, leaving ¼ inch (6 mm) of space between each row. Then, tie 2 rows of decreasing alternating square knots, so you end with 1 square knot in the middle of each section.

10. In each of the 3 sections, divide the section in half, counting 6 cords in from one side, and join it with the adjacent section's 6 cords. This will create 3 new sections of 12 cords. In each of the three sections, leaving a space of 3 inches (7.5 cm) below the third last row of alternating square knots, tie 1 row of 3 diagonal alternating square knots that angle down and to the left with a ¹⁄₁₆-inch (1.5-mm) space between each knot. Back under the first square knot you just tied, tie a row of 2 diagonal alternating square knots angling down and to the right with the same spacing.

11. In each of the 3 sections, using all 12 cords, tie the top half of a double half hitch diamond tight to the square knots above (page 155).

12. In each of the 3 sections; tie a macadamia knot (page 137) in the middle of the half diamond.

12

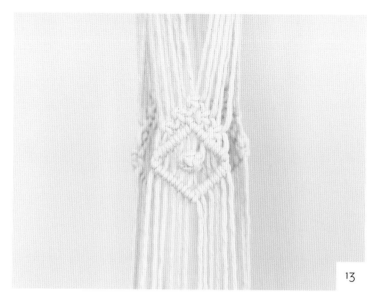

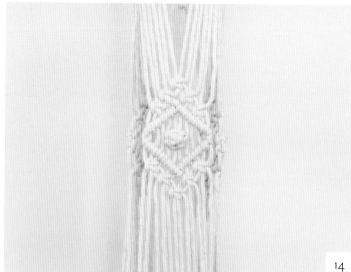

13. In each of the 3 sections, tie the bottom half of the double half hitch diamond using all 12 cords.

14. In each of the 3 sections, on the left side of the double half hitch diamond, tie a row of 2 diagonal alternating square knots with a 1/16-inch (1.5-mm) space between each knot, angling down and to the right, tight to the row above. On the right side of the diamond, in each of the three sections, tie a row of 3 diagonal alternating square knots, angling down and to the left with the same spacing. This will join the square knot rows.

15. Hold one of the wrapped 5-inch (13-cm) rings 2½ inches (6.5 cm) below the last knots. In each of the 3 sections, tie it in place with 12 double half hitches all next to each other, but leaving an even space of 2⅜ inches (6 cm) between each section. Try to hide the end of the string from the wrapped double half hitch ends under one of the knotted sections. Also try to keep the hoop level from each angle. You will be tying double half hitches on top of the already wrapped ring.

16. Group each section into their original 3 sections of 12 strands from step 8. With the middle 4 cords in each section, tie 1 square knot 1½ inches (4 cm) down from the hoop. In each section, tie 2 rows of increasing alternating square knots with ¼ inch (6 mm) of space between each row.

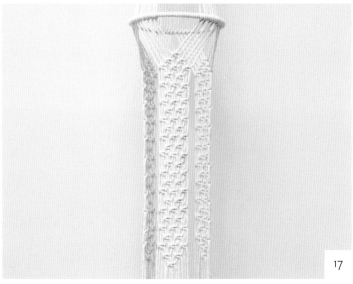

17

18

19

17. In each of the 3 sections, tie 20 rows of alternating square knots, leaving ¼ inch (6 mm) of space between each row. Tie 2 rows of decreasing alternating square knots, so you end with 1 square knot in the middle of each section.

18. Divide each of the 3 sections in half, counting 6 cords in from one side, and join them with the adjacent section's 6 cords to create 3 new sections of 12 cords. In each of the 3 sections, leaving a space of 3 inches (7.5 cm) below the third last row of alternating square knots, tie 1 row of 3 diagonal alternating square knots that angle down and to the left with ¹⁄₁₆ inch (1.5 mm) of space between each knot. Back under the first square knot you just tied, tie a row of 2 diagonal alternating square knots angling down and to the right with the same spacing.

19. In each of the 3 sections, tie half of a double half hitch diamond using all 12 cords, tight to the square knots above.

20. In each of the 3 sections, again tie a macadamia knot in the middle of the half diamond.

20

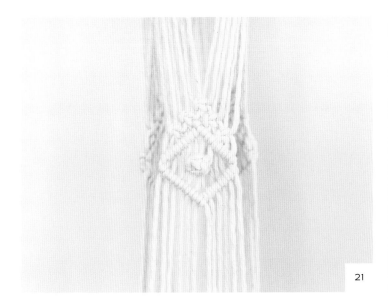
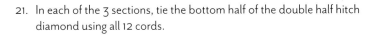

21. In each of the 3 sections, tie the bottom half of the double half hitch diamond using all 12 cords.

22. In each of the 3 sections, on the right side, tie 1 row of 2 diagonal alternating square knots with 1/16 inch (1.5 mm) of space between each knot, angling down and to the left, tight to the row above. On the left side of the diamond, tie a row of 3 diagonal alternating square knots, angling down and to the right with the same spacing. This will join the square knots.

23. Group each section into their original 3 sections of 12 strands from step 16. Measuring 3 inches (7.5 cm) down from the last square knot, tie one of the wrapped 5-inch (13-cm) rings in place with 12 double half hitches all next to each other, but leaving an even space of 2⅜ inches (6 cm) between each section. Try to hide the double half hitch ends on the wrapped hoop under one of the knotted sections. Also try to keep the hoop level from each angle.

24. In each of the 3 sections, measuring ¾ inch (2 cm) from the hoop, tie a cluster of 4 square knots.

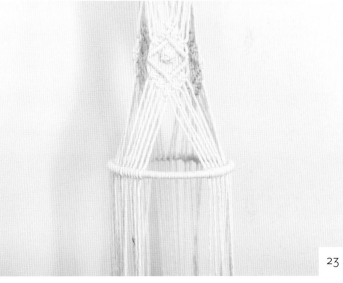

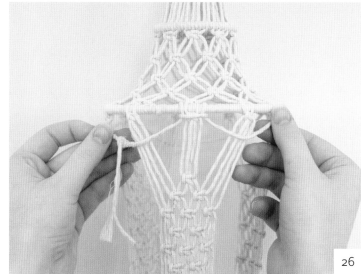

25. Cut 1 piece of ⁵⁄₆₄-inch (2-mm) single-strand string, 4 feet (1.2 m) long. Tie a gathering knot that is 1¾ inches (4.5 cm) long, 1 inch (2.5 cm) from the last knot. Cut the cords so they hang 18 inches (46 cm) from the top of the gathering knot.

26. Cut 3 pieces of ⁵⁄₆₄-inch (2-mm) single-strand string, 3 feet (92 cm) long. With one of these pieces, leaving a tail of 6¾ inches (17 cm) on the top 5-inch (13-cm) ring, tie a continuous lark's head knot (page 150) in the 3 sections shown in the photo. When tying, measure 5¼ inches (13 cm) over on the strand of continuous lark's head knots and tie another continuous lark's head knot in the next section shown. Repeat this one more time in the next section, so that you've tied a total of 3 continuous lark's head knots evenly spaced apart. Tie a reef knot (page 135) with both ends of the string, leaving a 3-inch (7.5-cm) tail on both of the ends. Each swoop at its middle point hangs down off the hoop by 1¼ inches (3 cm). This will let you attach the cords to make the fringe.

27. Using one of the other 3-foot (92-cm) cords you cut in the previous step, repeat step 26 on the middle 5-inch (13-cm) ring.

28

29

30

28. Using the last 3-foot (92-cm) cord from step 26, on the last 5-inch (13-cm) ring, leave a tail of 6¾ inches (17 cm) and tie a continuous lark's head knot in the middle of the 2-inch (5-cm) openings between the double half hitches which secured the ring (shown in the photo). Measuring 6 inches (15 cm) over, tie another continuous lark's head knot in the middle of the next opening; repeat this one more time in the next opening. Tie a reef knot with both ends of the rope, leaving a 3¼-inch (8-cm) tail on both of the ends from the reef knot. Each swoop at its middle point hangs down off the hoop by 1½ inches (4 cm).

29. Cut 432 pieces of ⁵⁄₆₄-inch (2-mm) single-strand rope, 7½ inches (19 cm) long. I suggest wrapping the rope around a piece of cardboard cut to 7½ inches (19 cm) and then cutting along both edges of the cardboard, through the string. This is a faster method for cutting this many small strands of string (similar method to making a pompom in knitting). Fold each piece in half and attach 16 pieces to each swooped section you just attached in steps 26, 27 and 28.

30. Brush out the 3 layers of fringe with a slicker brush (page 159) or by whatever method you prefer. Trim the fringe sections to clean up the ends.

Find your favorite plants and place them in the two openings and enjoy! Install the plant hanger on a strongly mounted curtain rod or a ceiling hook which can support the weight of the macramé plus your potted plants. I especially recommend that you weigh your own finished piece with the plants in it. See page 10 for an easy way to weigh large macramé pieces.

DAHLIA ROUND RUG

This is a project for those of you who are feeling ambitious and want to tackle a piece of functional macramé art that will have a huge payoff! I'm not going to lie, this project took a lot of time to design and complete, but I was so determined to include it in this book because of how gorgeous the results were. I love everything about this rug, and so do my cats, who all enjoy lying on it! Plan to work on this project over the course of a few weeks (or your own timeline) to break it down into manageable pieces of time. For example, make one floral circle a night while watching a TV series or listening to a podcast or audiobook. I personally love having a large project to chip away at and come back to over a period of time because it can be relaxing to work on something that's slow and repetitive. And doesn't that always make the end result even sweeter?

skill level: expert

DIMENSIONS
3 feet 10 inches (117 cm) in diameter (including fringe)

MATERIALS AND TOOLS
About 3,385 feet (1,031.7 m) of ⅛-inch (3-mm) single-strand string

Large-eye needle

Fabric glue (I used Aleene's Original Tacky Glue since it's all purpose and nontoxic)

Slicker brush

KNOTS USED
Reverse Lark's Head Knot (page 128)

Double Half Hitch/Free Floating Double Half Hitch (page 154)

Continuous Lark's Head Knot (page 150)

Reef Knot (page 135)

Tips before you start:

Since this is a rug, it will get a lot of wear; I suggest using a dab of fabric glue on each of the cords sewn into the back of the rug so that it holds up better. Also tie your knots nice and tight so they hold their shape over time. Keep in mind it will need to be treated with care since it's handmade. Spot wash with a mild clear soap or, if it will be in a high traffic or spill-prone area, try making it with a darker color.

You should cut the rope as needed in each step, based on the chart on the next page, rather than all at the beginning because as the center circle gets bigger, it takes longer to complete each row. This way you can stop and take a break and set it aside for later without worrying about mixing up all of the precut rope lengths.

These steps in the center circle can get repetitive, which is why there are only 9 photos. Once you get the concept, it's the same steps repeated; only the rope lengths and numbers change. Do your best to follow along, mainly paying attention to the changing rope lengths and number of working cords added. Don't worry too much about the exact number of double half hitch knots being the same in each row—as long as it's close. If you accidentally miss a rope and only notice a few rows later, don't worry, just keep going and sew that into the back later. Your goal is to make an 18¼-inch (46-cm) flat circle and avoid letting it curl up.

notes:

On the row where you are adding rope or the row right after rope is added, the knots will need to be tied very tight together and slightly squished so they fit around the row. Hold the filler cords and pull on the knots to squish them together every now and again.

On each row, offset your filler cord by the circumference of the circle, so the ends of the cord are even lengths.

REFER TO THIS CHART FOR YOUR PATTERN DETAILS

Refer to this chart first for each row for the required rope amount, lengths and other details discussed below.

Row Number: This indicates which row requires what (*be careful not to mix up the step numbers with the row numbers*).

Filler Cord Length: Filler cord indicates the cord being used around the circumference of each row, and the knots are being tied around this cord. *Make sure to offset and position the filler cord so you have even tails left over, because they will become working cords in the next row.*

Number of New Working Cords and Lengths: This indicates how many cords you need to cut, at what length. These cords will be used to increase the diameter of your piece and will be used when you are asked to "add new rope every xx knots."

Add Rope Every Specified Number of Knots: This number indicates how many knots you should tie on this row before adding a "new working cord" to the filler cord, using a reverse lark's head knot. *Note: On some rows there are an uneven number of knots, so add the indicated number of "new working cords" until you've used them all, and on some rows there will be a random amount of cords left, so just continue tying your knots till the end of the row.*

Total Double Half Hitches Tied: This indicates the number of double half hitches you will have in each row. As mentioned previously, don't worry if your numbers end up slightly different, as long as your circle stays flat and ends up the right diameter. These are here for reference.

"-": Indicates that this column is not applicable in this step.

Row Number	Filler Cord Length	Number of New Working Cords and Lengths	Add Rope Every Specified Number of Knots	Total Double Half Hitches Tied
1	-	6 x 132 inches (335.5 cm)	Every cord	0
2	132 inches (335.5 cm)	-	-	16
3	132 inches (335.5 cm)	-	-	16
4	120 inches (305 cm)	6 x 120 inches (305 cm)	3	18
5	120 inches (305 cm)	-	-	32
6	104 inches (264 cm)	10 x 104 inches (264 cm)	3	34
7	104 inches (264 cm)	-	-	58
8	104 inches (264 cm)	-	-	58
9	96 inches (244 cm)	10 x 96 inches (244 cm)	6	60
10	96 inches (244 cm)	-	-	80
11	96 inches (244 cm)	13 x 96 inches (244 cm)	6	82
12	84 inches (213 cm)	-	-	110
13	84 inches (213 cm)	-	-	112
14	84 inches (213 cm)	12 x 70 inches (178 cm)	9	114
15	84 inches (213 cm)	-	-	138
16	84 inches (213 cm)	14 x 70 inches (178 cm)	9	140
17	84 inches (213 cm)	-	-	172
18	96 inches (244 cm)	-	-	174
19	96 inches (244 cm)	8 x 72 inches (183 cm)	20	176
20	96 inches (244 cm)	-	-	193
21	96 inches (244 cm)	9 x 72 inches (183 cm)	20	195
22	96 inches (244 cm)	-	-	216
23	96 inches (244 cm)	-	-	218
24	96 inches (244 cm)	8 x 60 inches (152 cm)	25	220
25	96 inches (244 cm)	-	-	236
26	84 inches (213 cm)	13 x 36 inches (91 cm)	18	238
27	84 inches (213 cm)	-	-	267
28	78 inches (198 cm)	-	-	269
29	70 inches (178 cm)	-	-	271

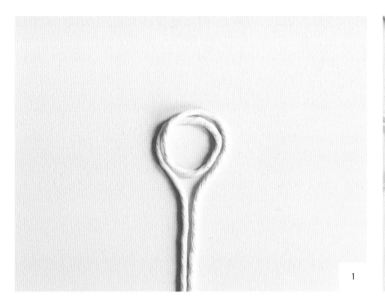

1

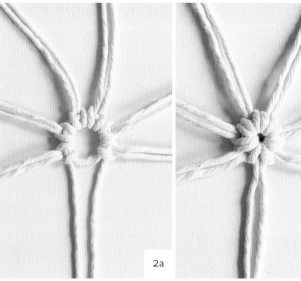

2a

2b

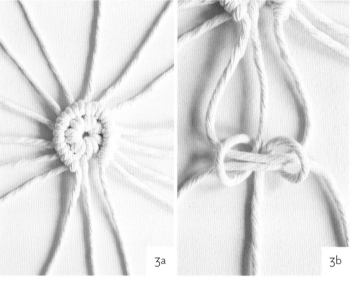

3a

3b

CREATING THE CENTER CIRCLE

1. Cut 1 piece of ⅛-inch (3-mm) single-strand string, 128 inches (325 cm) long. Find the center of the cord and at the center, coil it into a double circle (as pictured). You will be adding your first row around this coiled section. The long tails of this cord will become working cords.

2a. **Row 1:** Refer to the chart, and attach the other six 132-inch (335.5-cm) cords to the coiled double circle by folding each cord in half and attaching with a reverse lark's head knot.

2b. Pull tight on both long tails from the coiled double circle so that it tightens the circle and each cord is tight next to each other. Treat both of these tails like working cords going forward.

3a. **Row 2:** Continue referring to the chart for this step and the following ones.

3b. Tie a full row of double half hitches around the circumference. Tie your last double half hitch around both ends of your filler cord.

3c. Pull tight; this creates 1 continuous row of double half hitches. The tails of the filler cords will be treated as working cords for the next row.

3c

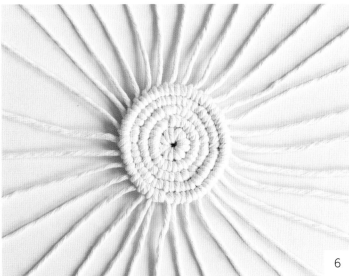

4. **Row 3:** Tie a full row of double half hitches, ending by tying the last knot around both ends of the filler cord as shown in previous step photos 3b and 3c.

5. **Row 4:** Tie a full row of double half hitches, and add rope every few knots as indicated by the chart, ending by tying the last knot around both ends of the filler cord.

6. **Row 5:** Tie a full row of double half hitches, ending by tying the last knot around both ends of the filler cord.

7. **Row 6:** Tie a full row of double half hitches, and add rope every few knots as indicated by the chart, ending by tying the last knot around both ends of the filler cord.

8

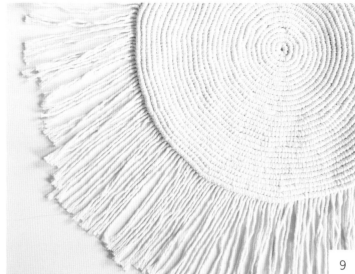

9

10

8. **Row 7:** Tie a full row of double half hitches, ending by tying the last knot around both ends of the filler cord.

9. Repeat steps 4 to 8, referring to the chart, until you have completed row 27. Tie a full row of double half hitches for rows 28 and 29, ending by tying the last knot around both ends of the filler cord.

MAKING THE SECOND LAYER FLORAL CIRCLES

Each circle is made up of 5 rows. Each row will have several steps involved, so make sure to pay attention to the headings and steps to stay on track. Also, do your best to keep your knots and tension in each row the same for each circle, as this could affect the number of floral circles you need to surround the center circle. Keep referencing one completed floral circle as you work to make sure the scale is the same and you are on track. One of my completed floral circles is approximately 8 inches (20 cm) in diameter.

row 1

10. To prep for Row 1, cut 1 piece of ⅛-inch (3-mm) single-strand string, 16 inches (41 cm) long. This is your central filler cord. Cut 1 piece of ⅛-inch (3-mm) single-strand string, 4 feet (1.2 m) long. This is your Row 1 filler cord. Cut 2 pieces of ⅛-inch (3-mm) single-strand string, 42 inches (107 cm) long. These are your Row 1 working cords. Take your 16-inch (41-cm) central filler cord and coil it into a double circle (as pictured). You will be adding your first row around this coiled cord. Set it aside for now.

11 . Leave a 5-inch (13-cm) tail at the beginning of each cord. *Using a 42-inch (107-cm) Row 1 working cord, tie a double half hitch around your 4-foot (1.2-m) Row 1 filler cord.* Repeat between * * with your second Row 1 working cord.

11

12

13

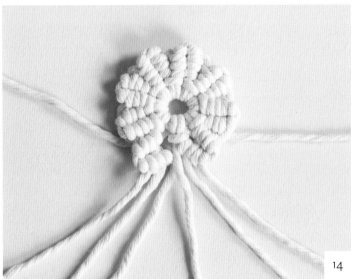

14

12. Fold over your Row 1 filler cord and tie 1 double half hitch using each of the Row 1 working cords.

13. Attach the long tail end of your Row 1 filler cord to your coiled central filler cord using a continuous lark's head knot. Use a large-eye needle to tie the continuous lark's head knot if you find it easier. This completes 1 petal.

14. Tie 7 more completed petals around the coiled central filler cord, making sure to finish with a continuous lark's head knot using your Row 1 filler cord. Pull tight on your double circle tails to tighten.

15a. Turn the piece over and using a large-eye needle, sew each end into the back of the knots in the direction they are traveling to complete the pattern, so that the ends are secure. The exact placement doesn't matter, as long as it is secure and the front looks good.

15b. Trim the excess and put a small dab of fabric glue on the end of each cord. Finished Row 1 measures 2⅜ inches (6 cm) in diameter.

15a

15b

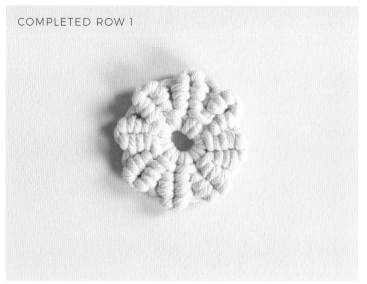

17

row 2

16. To prep for Row 2, cut 1 piece of ⅛-inch (3-mm) single-strand string, 5 feet (1.5 m) long. This is your Row 2 filler cord. Cut 2 pieces of ⅛-inch (3-mm) single-strand string, 7 feet (2.1 m) long. These are your Row 2 working cords.

17. Leave a 5-inch (13-cm) tail at the beginning of each cord. *Using a 7-foot (2.1-m) Row 2 working cord, tie a double half hitch around your 5-foot (1.5-m) Row 2 filler cord.* Repeat between * * with your second Row 2 working cord.

18. Fold over your Row 2 filler cord and tie 1 double half hitch using each of the Row 2 working cords.

19. Fold over your Row 2 filler cord and tie 1 double half hitch using each of the Row 2 working cords. Again, fold over your Row 2 filler cord and tie 1 double half hitch using each of the Row 2 working cords. You now have a group of 2 petals.

18

19

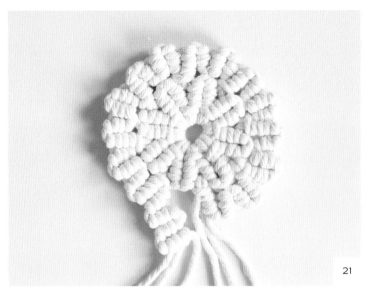

20. Using a large-eye needle, attach the long tail of your Row 2 filler cord to the small space between 2 petals using a continuous lark's head knot. This completes 2 petals in Row 2.

21. Tie 14 more completed petals as described above (in groups of 2) for a total of 16 petals in Row 2. After tying your group of 2 petals, secure it to Row 1 by tying a continuous lark's head knot in between every petal from Row 1, making sure to finish with a continuous lark's head knot using your Row 2 filler cord.

22a. Turn the piece over and, using a large-eye needle, sew each end into the back of the knots in the direction they are traveling to complete the pattern, so that the ends are secure. It doesn't have to be in these exact spots, as long as it is secure and the front looks good.

22b. Trim the excess and put a small dab of fabric glue on the end of each cord. Finished Row 2 measures 3¾ inches (10 cm) in diameter.

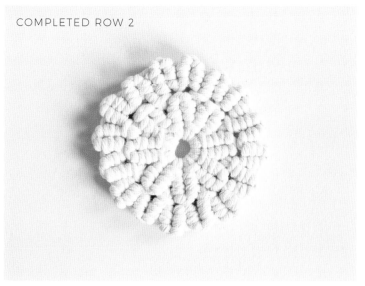

24

row 3

23. To prep for Row 3, cut 1 piece of ⅛-inch (3-mm) single-strand string, 6 feet (1.8 m) long. This is your Row 3 filler cord. Cut 2 pieces of ⅛-inch (3-mm) single-strand string, 9 feet (2.7 m) long. These are your Row 3 working cords.

24. Leave a 5-inch (13-cm) tail at the beginning of each cord. *Using a 9-foot (2.7-m) Row 3 working cord, tie a double half hitch around your 6-foot (1.8-m) Row 3 filler cord.* Repeat between ** with your second Row 3 working cord.

25. *Fold over your Row 3 filler cord and tie 1 double half hitch using each of the Row 3 working cords.* Repeat between ** 4 more times. You now have a group of 3 petals.

26. Using a large-eye needle, attach the long end of your Row 3 filler cord using a continuous lark's head knot to the small space between 2 petals. This completes 3 petals in Row 3.

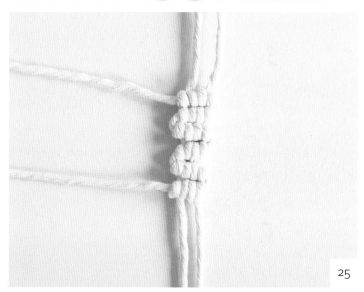

25

26

27

28a

28b

COMPLETED ROW 3

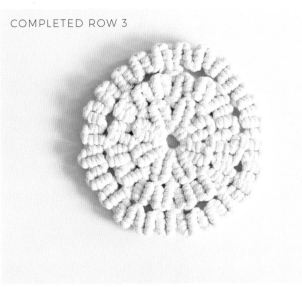

27. Tie 21 more completed petals as described above (in groups of 3) for a total of 24 petals in Row 3. After tying your group of 3 petals, secure it to Row 2 by tying a continuous lark's head knot in between every petal from Row 2, making sure to finish with a continuous lark's head knot using your Row 3 filler cord.

28a. Turn the piece over and, using a large-eye needle, sew each end into the back of the knots in the direction they are traveling to complete the pattern, so that the ends are secure. It doesn't have to be in these exact spots, as long as it is secure and the front looks good.

28b. Trim the excess and put a small dab of fabric glue on the end of each cord. Finished Row 3 measures between 5 and 5¼ inches (approximately 13 cm) in diameter.

row 4

29. To prep for Row 4, cut 1 piece of ⅛-inch (3-mm) single-strand string, 8 feet (2.4 m) long. This is your Row 4 filler cord. Cut 2 pieces of ⅛-inch (3-mm) single-strand string, 11½ feet (3.5 m) long. These are your Row 4 working cords.

30. Leave a 5-inch (13-cm) tail at the beginning of each cord. *Using an 11½-foot (3.5-m) Row 4 working cord, tie a double half hitch around your 8-foot (2.4-m) Row 4 filler cord.* Repeat between * * with your second Row 4 working cord.

30

31

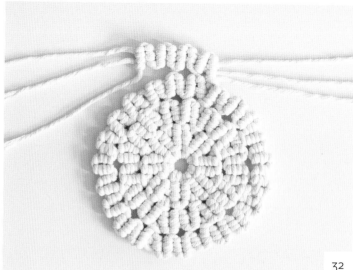

32

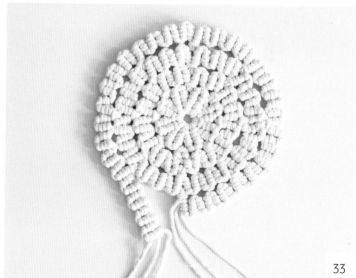

33

31. *Fold over your Row 4 filler cord and tie 1 double half hitch using each of the Row 4 working cords.* Repeat between ** 6 more times. You now have a group of 4 petals.

32. Using a large-eye needle, attach the long tail end of your Row 4 filler cord to the small space between 2 petals using a continuous lark's head knot. This completes 4 petals in Row 4.

33. Tie 28 more completed petals as described above for a total of 32 petals in Row 4. After tying your group of 3 petals, secure it to Row 3 by tying a continuous lark's head knot in between every petal from Row 3, making sure to finish with a continuous lark's head knot using your Row 4 filler cord.

34a. Turn the piece over and, using a large-eye needle, sew each end into the back of the knots in the direction they are traveling to complete the pattern, so that the ends are secure. It doesn't have to be in these exact spots, as long as it is secure and the front looks good.

34b. Trim the excess and put a small dab of fabric glue on the end of each cord. Finished Row 4 measures 6½ inches (17 cm) in diameter.

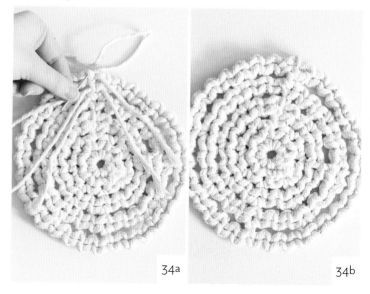

34a

34b

COMPLETED ROW 4

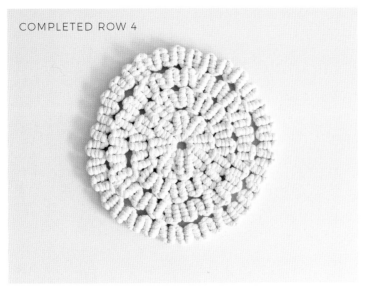

36

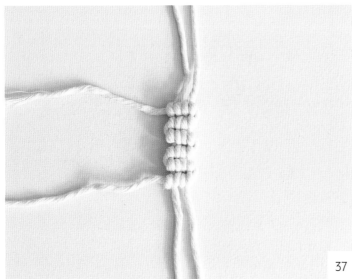

37

row 5

35. To prep for Row 5, cut 1 piece of ⅛-inch (3-mm) single-strand string, 11 feet (3.3 m) long. This is your Row 5 filler cord. Cut 2 pieces of ⅛-inch (3-mm) single-strand string, 15 feet (4.5 m) long. These are your Row 5 working cords.

36. Leave a 5-inch (13-cm) tail at the beginning of each cord. *Using a 15-foot (4.5-m) Row 5 working cord, tie a double half hitch around your 11-foot (3.3-m) Row 5 filler cord.* Repeat between * * with your second Row 5 working cord.

37. *Fold over your Row 5 filler cord and tie 1 double half hitch using each of the Row 5 working cords.* Repeat between * * 6 more times. You now have a group of 3 petals.

38. Using a large-eye needle, attach the long end of your Row 4 filler cord to the small space between 3 petals using a continuous lark's head knot. This completes 3 petals in Row 5.

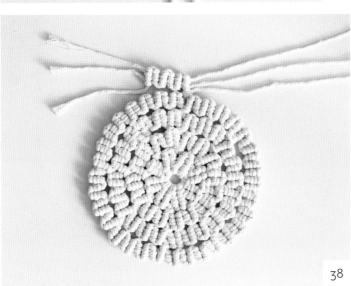

38

39

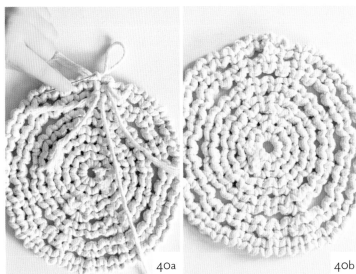

40a 40b

COMPLETED ROW 5

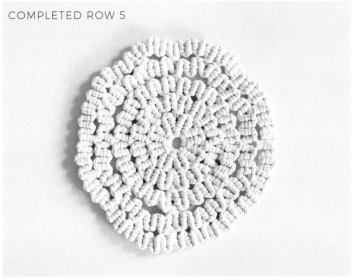

39. Tie 44 more completed petals as described above (in groups of 3) for a total of 47 petals in Row 5. After tying your group of 3 petals, secure it to Row 4 by tying a continuous lark's head knot in between every petal from Row 4, ending with a grouping of 2 petals and a continuous lark's head knot using your Row 5 filler cord.

40a. Turn the piece over and, using a large-eye needle, sew each end into the back of the knots in the direction they are traveling to complete the pattern, so that the ends are secure. It doesn't have to be in these exact spots, as long as it is secure and the front looks good.

40b. Trim the excess and put a small dab of fabric glue on the end of each cord. Finished Row 5 measures 8 inches (20 cm) in diameter.

41. Repeat steps 10 to 40 (Rows 1 to 5) 9 more times, so you have a total of 10 floral circles.

41

42

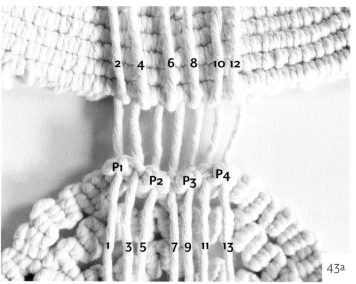

43a

43b

ATTACHING THE SECOND LAYER FLORAL CIRCLES TO THE CENTER CIRCLE

42. Lay the center circle down on the floor or other large flat surface, and arrange the second layer of floral circles around it so that there are 3 points of contact. Make sure all are touching the center circle and the circle on either side of itself. When arranging the second layer, try to line up any flatter edges of your floral circle as your point of contact with the center circle.

43a. On each floral circle, make 4 petals line up with 13 cords from the center circle where the second layer is making contact with the center. Using a large-eye needle, sew cord 1 up through P1, cord 3 between P1 and P2 and cord 5 through P2. Sew cord 7 between P2 and P3, cord 9 through P3, cord 11 between P3 and P4 and cord 13 through P4.

43b. Sew each cord listed above through its mentioned place, and then down in between the floral circle and center circle and into the back of two of the knots on the back of the rug. Sew cords 2, 4, 6, 8, 10 and 12 into the back of two double half hitch knots in the center circle. Make sure to pull tight on each cord for a tight and secure seam. Trim the excess cord and put a small dab of fabric glue on the end of each cord.

Repeat this to each of the 10 second layer floral circles.

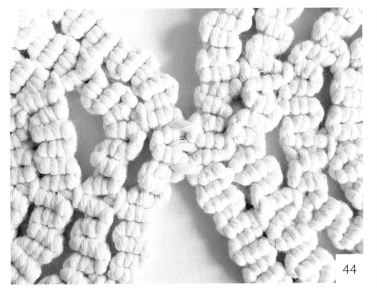

44

45

46

44. Cut 10 pieces of ⅛-inch (3-mm) single-strand string, at 15 inches (38 cm) long. Sew 3 stiches between each of the floral circles in the second layer. Sew the 2 ends into the back of the double half hitches of the second layer of circles. Trim the excess cord and put a small dab of fabric glue on the end of each cord.

45. Sew each cord coming out of the center circle into the back of itself, through the back of 2 double half hitches. Trim the excess and put a small dab of fabric glue on the end of each cord.

MAKING THE THIRD OUTER LAYER

46. Cut 1 piece of ⅛-inch (3-mm) single-strand string, 159 inches (404 cm) long. Using a large-eye needle, leave a 6-inch (15-cm) tail and attach the cord with a continuous lark's head knot to the edge of one of the floral circles, centered in between one of the petals from the second row.

47. Using the 159-inch (404-cm) cord from the previous step, measure 11 inches (28 cm) over and attach it with a continuous lark's head knot to the middle edge of the next floral circle, in between 2 petals. Repeat this step 9 more times so your cord goes around the diameter of the rug. Your last continuous lark's head knot will be attached in between the same petals at the first one in the previous step.

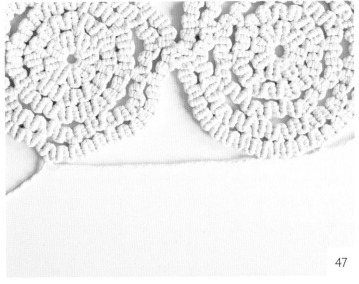

47

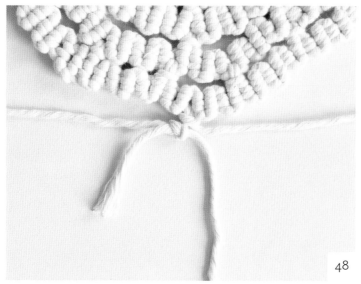

48

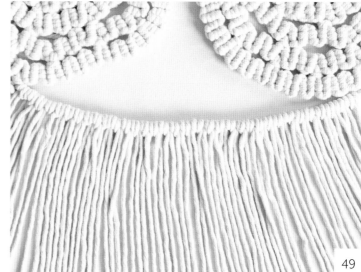

49

50

48. Tie the two tails from the continuous lark's head knots together with a reef knot and sew the ends into the back of the second layer floral circles. Trim and add a dab of glue to the ends.

49. Cut 360 pieces of ⅛-inch (3-mm) single-strand string, at 40 inches (102 cm) each. To make cutting these faster, you can wrap the rope 180 times around a piece of cardboard that is 40 inches long, and cut through the rope along both edges of cardboard (similar method to making a pompom in knitting. See photo 29 on page 63 for reference in a smaller size). Attach 36 cords per section between each continuous lark's head knot by folding in half and tying a reverse lark's head knot. If 36 cords are too tight in a section, you can alter this to fit the section.

50. Cut 5 pieces of ⅛-inch (3-mm) single-strand string, at 142 inches (361 cm) each. These will be your filler cords. Leaving a tail of 10 inches (25 cm) with each filler cord, tie 5 rows of double half hitches with each of the cords you just attached around the entire diameter of the rug. When you complete one row, use a large-eye needle to insert the filler cord through the middle of the double half hitch beside it to secure it, and treat it as the working cord for the fringe in the next step.

51. Trim all of the working cords to 4 inches (10 cm) or your preferred length around the diameter of the rug. This will be the fringe. Brush out the trimmed cords with a slicker brush (page 159). You can also get creative here and braid the working cords before cutting to create thick tassels, sew in the cords so there is no fringe, or whatever you would like!

You're finally done! Place where you would like in your home and enjoy all of your hard work! See page 65 for tips on use and care.

51

backdrops & CURTAINS

As an art form, macramé can often be put inside a box, constrained to only hanging on walls or holding plants. I love to push the limits with macramé when it comes to both style and purpose. One of the ways this chapter does that is through the room divider (page 85) and door curtain projects (page 105). Macramé looks amazing when you take it off the wall and use it in these ways because of its delicately light and airy patterns. They're both the perfect combination of style and function, and I can envision them completing the look of a house, office or any other location that could benefit from some light separation of spaces!

Macramé backdrops are some of the most sought-after pieces of décor for weddings because they can match so many different design themes and have an indescribable ability to elevate a couple's big day. The backdrop designs in this chapter are of course great for weddings, but they can also be used for bridal showers, baby showers, special events, feature walls, photoshoots or anything else you can dream up. I've used macramé backdrops in each of those situations and it never ceases to make the event extra special, draw lots of compliments from guests and make for gorgeous memorable photos. I personally love creating designs for the special days in people's lives. I'm so glad to share these projects with you for the special moments in your life!

TRELLIS ROOM DIVIDER

I have always been in love with the idea of a macramé room divider, so I knew I had to design one to share in this book. I love the look of a simplistic design when it is blown up and oversized. The pattern creates an eye-catching feature and doesn't take up any visual space as the design is very open and see-through. In theory, this piece seems easy to create, as it only uses alternating square knots with large spaces between them. In reality, when you leave large spaces between knots, you have to be even more accurate with your placement. With this piece, take your time tying the knots very precisely so that the knots are all the same size and tied with the same strength each time. Make sure that each knot is the same size and height as the other knots in that row by using a measuring tape each time. The room divider will be much more striking if it's precise and accurate than if the knots are all over the place. This piece will help strengthen your precision and fine-tune your accuracy!

Tips: If you would like to alter the piece's width to be larger or smaller, work in increments of 4 strands of rope and follow the same steps. Note about the height for installing—this piece is meant be installed with a little tension on the cords. Adjust the height accordingly; otherwise make it to just hang freely by leaving out the eye screws on the bottom piece of wood.

Make sure to stand back and get perspective throughout the making of the piece. Even if a knot is tied at the right height, it might still feel off, and by standing back you may notice that the knot above it is slightly off, which will also affect the knot you just tied. This approach helps to keep your work as even as possible.

No drill, no problem!

If you don't have access to a drill, you can simply attach the rope to the piece of wood using a lark's head knot on a slightly longer piece of wood, instead of threading the rope through the drilled holes. Simply leave out steps 1 and 2, and start from step 3 using a lark's head knot and dowel instead. Leave the rope at the bottom to hang freely without adding wood at the bottom.

skill level: intermediate

DIMENSIONS
45⅛ inches (114.5 cm) wide (wood width) x 8 feet (2.5 m) high

MATERIALS AND TOOLS
1 wood piece (oak or another hard wood) 90¼ inches (229 cm) long x ¾ inch (2 cm) long x ½ inch (1.3 cm) thick

Saw to cut the wood (or have it cut at the hardware store before bringing it home)

5/16-inch (8-mm) drill bit

Drill

Scrap wood to drill into

Safety goggles

Wood punch and hammer (optional)

7/64-inch (3-mm) drill bit, or size to match screw eyes

Masking tape

4 (1⅝-inch [41-mm]) medium screw eyes

Pliers

About 632 feet (193 m) of 9/32-inch (7-mm) sash or braided rope (I used sash rope)

Measuring tape

4 (2½-inch [6.5-cm]) screw hooks

KNOTS USED
Square Knot (page 130)

Alternating Square Knot (page 143)

Overhand Knot (page 134)

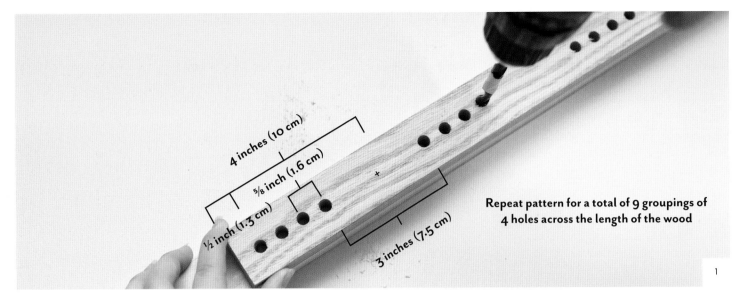

4 inches (10 cm)

⅝ inch (1.6 cm)

½ inch (1.3 cm)

3 inches (7.5 cm)

Repeat pattern for a total of 9 groupings of 4 holes across the length of the wood

1

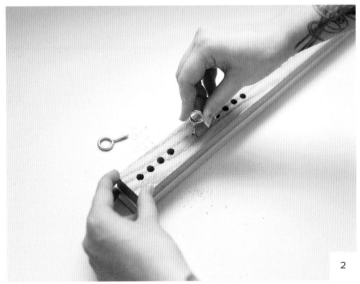

2

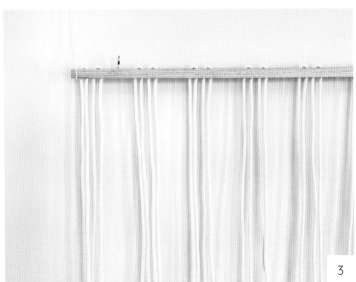

3

1. Cut the piece of wood in half so both pieces are 45⅛ inches (114.5 cm) long. On both pieces, mark the drill holes based on the diagram and drill the marked holes with a ⁵⁄₁₆-inch (8-mm) drill bit. The drill bit should be the same size as the rope you use, so it threads perfectly through the holes. Make sure to have a scrap piece of wood underneath your piece of wood to drill into. This creates clean holes in the piece you're going to use. Make sure to wear safety goggles while cutting and drilling. Optional: To keep your drill bit from moving as you are starting the hole, you can use a wood punch and hammer to create a divot into the piece of wood. This is a small guide to help the tip of the drill bit from slipping.

2. On the first piece of wood, using a ⁷⁄₆₄-inch (3-mm) drill bit (or a drill bit the right size for your screw eyes), drill a hole only halfway through in the spots marked with a + for the screw eyes. I find it helpful to use masking tape to mark the drill bit with the maximum height you want to drill into the wood. This way you don't accidentally drill a hole all the way through. Screw the eye screws into the holes by hand or with pliers. Repeat for the second piece of wood.

3. Cut 2 pieces of ⁹⁄₃₂-inch (7-mm) sash rope, each 28 feet (8.5 m) long and 16 pieces of ⁹⁄₃₂-inch (7-mm) sash rope, each 36 feet (11 m) long. Make sure to cut each strand using masking tape (page 9) to keep the ends from fraying and so it is easier to thread through the wood. Thread one of the 28-foot (8.5-m) pieces through the far left 2 holes. Position the rope so that 28 feet (8.5 m) of rope is threaded through the left hole and 10 feet (3 m) through the second hole from the left end.

Do the same on the right side but with 10 feet (3 m) threaded through the second hole from the left and the 28 feet (8.5 m) threaded through the last right hole. Thread the remaining 16 pieces through each of the holes so they are all even lengths, so there is 18 feet (5.5 m) coming through each of the holes.

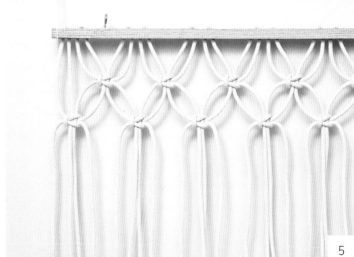

4

5

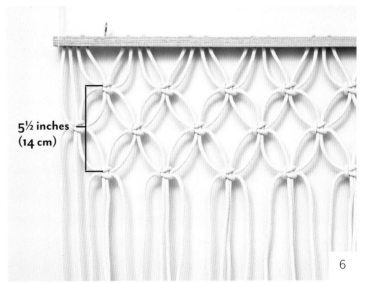

5½ inches
(14 cm)

6

4. Leaving out the first two cords on the left and the last two cords on the right, tie 1 row of 8 square knots 2¾ inches (7 cm) from the piece of wood across the divider. Make sure to use a measuring tape for each knot to make it more precise.

5. Using the two previously left out cords on either side of the divider, tie a row of 9 alternating square knots 6 inches (15 cm) from the piece of wood. To create rounded edges of rope in between the knots, slightly push up on the knot while holding the filler cords tight and slightly pull up on the working cords so the knot is positioned 5½ inches (14 cm) from the wood. This creates a rounder shape to the cord in between the knots compared to pulling the cords tight.

6. Tie a row of 8 alternating square knots 6 inches (15 cm) from the knot directly above (two rows above). Pull up on the working cords and push up on the knot very slightly to round the cords in the spaces so the knot ends up 5½ inches (14 cm) away from the knot above.

7. Continue 26 more rows of alternating square knots, leaving 5¼ inches (14 cm) of space between the knot directly above it (two rows above) and keeping the cords in between the knots rounded by using the method mentioned above.

Tip:

When tying, this can get quite long depending on the height of your setup; place the whole piece over the dowel, or clothes rack (like it is folded), so the top is hanging and adjust accordingly while working.

7

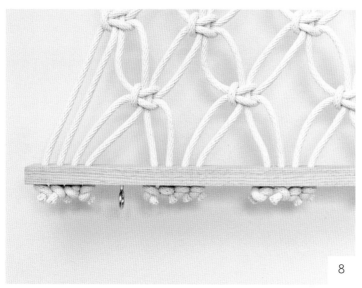

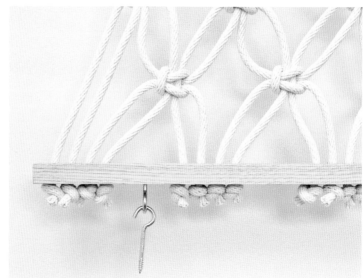

8

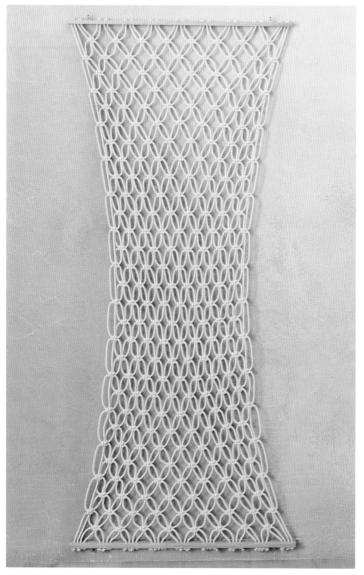

8. With the second piece of prepared and pre-drilled wood, thread each of the cords through the corresponding holes, making sure not to cross any cords. Position the piece of wood 2¾ inches (7 cm) down from the last row of knots and tie 1 overhand knot on the other side of the piece of wood. The wood should sit 2¾ inches (7 cm) down from the last row of knots so that the space between the top piece of wood and the bottom is about 8 feet (2.5 m). Trim any excess cord after the overhand knot, leaving about ³⁄₁₆ inch (5 mm) from the overhand knot.

installation tip:

Use screw hooks in the floor and ceiling that fit inside the eyehole, positioned the same width apart as the screw's eye. Make sure to screw the hooks into studs or anchors that will support its weight. See photo above for screw hook reference. My piece weighed 7⅕ pounds (3.2 kg), but to be safe you should always weigh your own finished piece. See page 10 for an easy way to weigh large macramé pieces. Note that if you make any adjustments to the project, it may change the weight. If you don't want to screw anything into the floor, leave out the screw eyes and hooks on the bottom piece of wood.

ANNALISE BACKDROP

What's dreamier than macramé as the backdrop to your wedding?! Its delicate, lace-like structure works perfectly as décor for those special days in your life like weddings, engagement parties, bridal or baby showers, or any event needing that impressive wow factor. If I could go back in time, macramé would obviously be at my wedding! This piece, though large, mainly uses half knots and square knots, which makes it a more approachable design, regardless of the many steps involved! I love seeing how you can push a design using fewer types of knots, especially because my natural inclination is to always add more details. You can take this backdrop to the next level by decorating the top of it with some greenery like Italian ruscus, eucalyptus or some florals!

Tips: Leave the panels' fringe long and slightly uneven. For a more dramatic look, do not cut as listed in step 12 and 18 and instead let the rope pile on the floor. This also helps if you're unsure of the height it will be hung at. Keep the cords you cut throughout this wall hanging to use for the fringe overlay. You can also use scrap rope from other pieces of macramé you've made. Stain the wood with a stain of your choice to match your other décor.

skill level: intermediate

DIMENSIONS
5 feet (1.5 m) wide x 6 feet (1.8 m) tall

MATERIALS AND TOOLS:
About 1,322 feet (403 m) of ³⁄₁₆-inch (5-mm) three-strand cotton rope

About 122 feet (37.2 m) of ³⁄₁₆-inch (5-mm) three-strand cotton rope (scrap rope if possible, see sizes needed in step 40)

1 wood piece 5 feet (1.5 m) long x ¾ inch (2 cm) wide x 2 inch (5 cm) thick (I used pine)

KNOTS USED
Lark's Head Knot (page 127)

Square Knot (page 130)

Alternating Square Knot (page 143)

Half Knot Sinnet (left- and right-facing) (page 141)

Gathering Knot (page 138)

Cluster of 3 and 4 Square Knots (page 148)

Square Knot with Multiple Filler and Working Cords (page 131)

Continuous Lark's Head Knot (page 150)

Overhand Knot (page 134)

Diagonal Alternating Square Knot (page 147)

1. Cut 20 strands of ³⁄₁₆-inch (5-mm) three-strand rope at 23 feet (7 m) long. Fold each cord in half and attach 10 cords with a lark's head knot to either side of the wood, 5½ inches (14 cm) in from the ends. These will be referred to as the left and right outer panels.

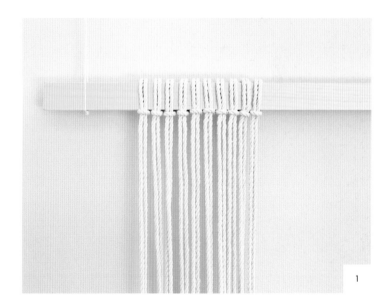

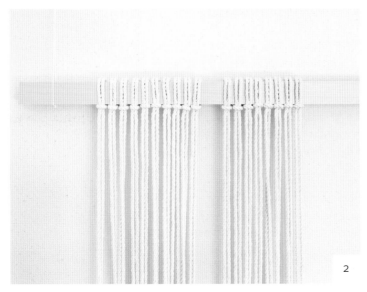

2

3

4

2. Cut 16 strands of ³⁄₁₆-inch (5-mm) three-strand rope at 20 feet (6 m) long. Fold each cord in half and attach 8 cords using a lark's head knot on the inside, on either side of the previous step's left and right outer panels. Leave a 1½-inch (4-cm) space between both panels. This is where the half knot sinnets will be added. These will be referred to as the left and right inner panels.

3. Cut 24 strands of ³⁄₁₆-inch (5-mm) three-strand rope at 12 feet (3.5 m) long. Fold each cord in half and attach all 24 cords using a lark's head knot in the middle of the piece of wood, leaving a 1½-inch (4-cm) space between the other cords from the left and right inner panels from the previous step. This is where the half knot sinnets will be added. This will be referred to as the center panel.

OUTER PANELS

Each step starts with you working on the left outer panel and tells you to repeat the same direction on the right panel.

4. Working from left to right, tie 2 square knots side by side with the first 8 cords, skip 4 cords, and tie 2 more square knots with the next 8 cords, all tight to the wood. Under both of these 2 square knots, tie 1 decreasing alternating square knot under both sets, tight to the knots above. With the middle four cords you skipped over, tie 6 right-facing half knot sinnets. Repeat these same steps on the right outer panel, but tie left-facing half knot sinnets instead.

5. Starting in the middle under the half knot sinnet, tie 1 row of 4 alternating square knots angling down and to the left and tie 1 row of 4 alternating square knots angling down and to the right. Repeat these same steps on the right outer panel.

5

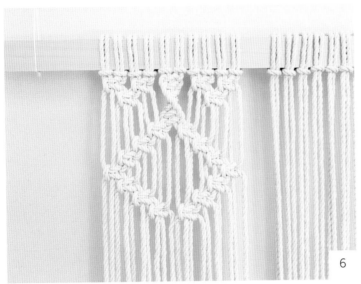

6. Starting under the square knots you just tied, tie 1 row of 3 alternating square knots angling down and toward the middle on both sides. Repeat these same steps on the right outer panel.

7. With the middle 4 cords (under the square knots you just tied), tie 12 right-facing half knots to create a 3¾-inch (9.5-cm)-long half knot sinnet. Repeat these same steps on the right outer panel, but tie a left-facing half knot sinnet instead.

8. With the outer 4 cords on both sides of the panel, tie 1 square knot 3 inches (7.5 cm) below the outer square knot above it. Working directly below your last knot, on both sides of the panel, tie 1 alternating square knot angling down and toward the middle of the panel itself, tight to the knot above. Working directly below your last knot, on either side of the panel, tie 1 alternating square knot angling down and outward with the outer 4 cords of the panel. Repeat these same steps on the right outer panel.

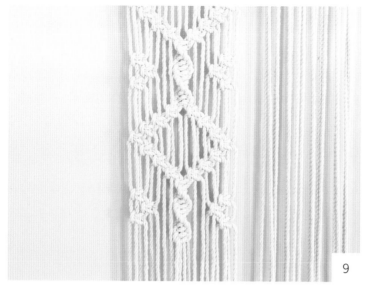

9

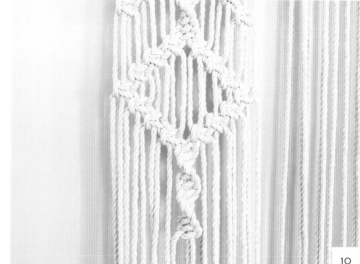

10

11

9. Repeat steps 5 to 8 two times.

10. Then repeat steps 5 to 7 once.

11. Cut 2 strands of ³⁄₁₆-inch (5-mm) three-strand rope at 62½ inches (159 cm). Under the half knot sinnets on both the outer panels, tie a gathering knot that is 1⅝ inches (4 cm) wide by leaving a tail of 37 inches (94 cm) to hang down with the other cords so it becomes a part of the fringe and then fold over and start wrapping.

12. Cut the cords from both outer panels at 6 feet (1.8 m) from the wood.

12

13

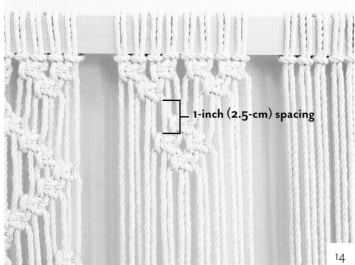

— 1-inch (2.5-cm) spacing

14

15

INNER PANELS

Each step starts with you working on the left inner panel and tells you to repeat the same direction on the right panel.

13. Working from left to right, tie a square knot, tight to the wood, with every 4 cords. This will create 1 row of 4 square knots. On the second row, skip 2 cords and tie an alternating square knot under and tight to the two square knots above. Skip 4 cords and tie another alternating square knot under and tight to the two square knots above. Repeat this on the right inner panel.

14. Working on the left inner panel, with the middle 4 cords, measuring 1 inch (2.5 cm) down from the last knots you tied in the previous step, tie a cluster of 4 square knots (page 148) all tight to each other. Repeat this on the right inner panel.

15. Working left to right, skip the first 2 cords and starting on the next 4 cords, measuring 1 inch (2.5 cm) down from the last knot you tied, tie a cluster of 4 square knots. Now working right to left, skip the first 2 cords and starting on the next 4 cords, tie a cluster of 4 square knots (page 148) at the same distance. Repeat this on the right inner panel.

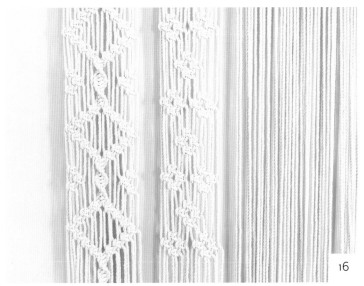

16

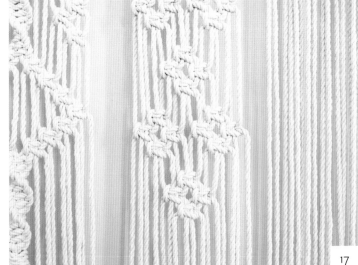

17

18

16. Repeat steps 14 and 15 four times on both inner panels.

17. Repeat step 14 one last time on both inner panels.

18. To trim the inner panel cords on an angle, cut the inner cord on both panels to 62½ inches (159 cm) and then cut diagonally starting from the shorter inner cord angling down and out to meet the 6-foot (183-cm) cord on the outer panel. This will create an even angle on both sides.

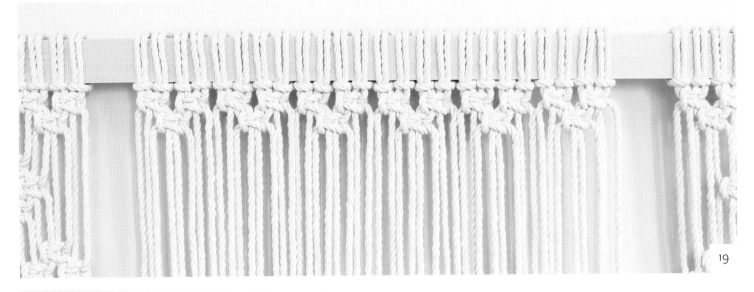

19

CENTER PANEL

19. Working left to right, tie 1 full row of square knots with every cord across the top and tight to the wood. On the next row, skip 2 cords in from the edge and tie an alternating square knot with the next 4 cords directly under and tight to the two square knots above. *Skip 4 cords, and tie another alternating square knot with the next 4 cords directly under and tight to the two square knots above.* Repeat between * * 4 more times until you get to the edge of the panel with just 2 cords left on the edge. This will help keep your cords in place and prevent the lark's head knots from easily moving around.

20. With the very middle 4 cords, measure 5¾ inches (14.5 cm) down from the bottom of the wood and tie 1 square knot.

21. Starting under the previous knot you just tied, tie 1 row of 10 alternating square knots on both sides, angling out toward the edge of the panel (leaving 2 cords on either side of the panel).

20

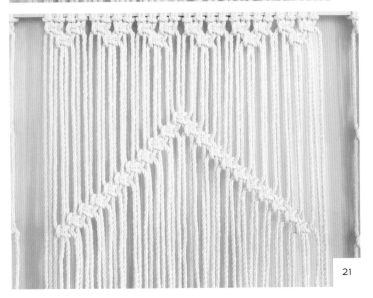

21

22

23

24

22. On the left side, with the first 4 cords, tie 5 right-facing half knots to create a half knot sinnet, tight to the knot above. Repeat this on the right side of the panel but with a left-facing half knot sinnet.

23. In the very middle of the center panel, starting 1 inch (2.5 cm) below the knot above it, tie another square knot. This is the top of the inner square knot diamond.

24. Starting under the previous knot you just tied, tie 1 row of 9 diagonal alternating square knots on both sides, angling out toward the edge of the panel.

25. Within the half diamond of square knots, tie a large square knot with 2 working cords on both sides and 20 filler cords centered within the half diamond. Make sure to tie the square knot loose enough that it does not make the filler cords overlap each other, but tight enough that it stays centered within the half diamond. This will leave 4 cords within the square knot diamond, on either side of the large square knot.

25

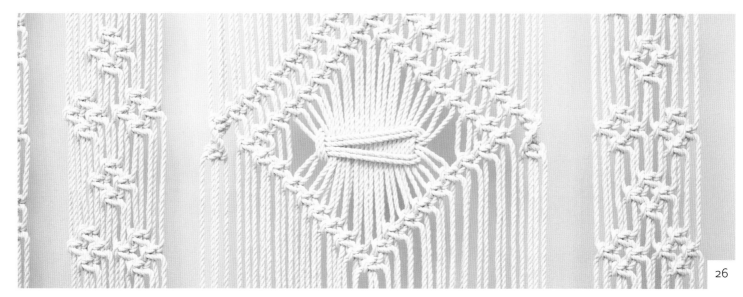

26

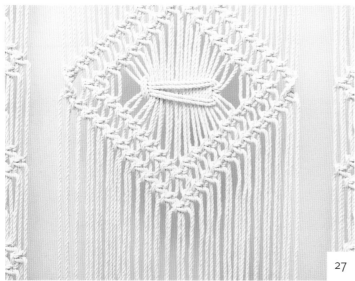

27

26. To close the half diamond, on the left side of the last square knot from the row you tied in step 24, tie 1 row of 8 alternating square knots angling down and to the right. Starting on the right side of the final square knot from step 24, tie 1 row of 9 alternating square knots angling down and toward the middle. This will close the inner square knot diamond. Make sure to use the corresponding cords coming from the large square knot and be mindful not to cross them and use the wrong one.

27. Under the half knot sinnets you tied in step 22, starting on the left side, leaving a space of 1 inch (2.5 cm), tie 1 row of 10 alternating square knots angling down and toward the center. On the right side, tie 1 row of 11 alternating square knots angling down and toward the center. This will complete the outer diamond.

28. Measuring down from the last row of knots, cut each of the cords to 10¾ inches (27 cm) long.

28

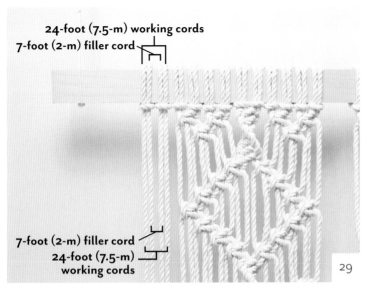

24-foot (7.5-m) working cords
7-foot (2-m) filler cord

7-foot (2-m) filler cord
24-foot (7.5-m) working cords

29

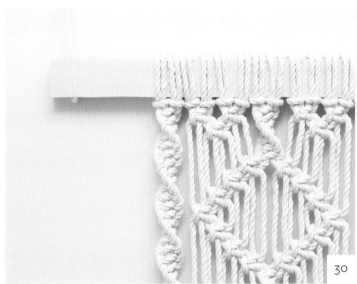

30

OUTER HALF KNOT SINNETS AND BETWEEN EACH PANEL

29. To make the outer half knot sinnets, cut 4 pieces of ³⁄₁₆-inch (5-mm) three-strand rope, 31 feet (9.5 m) long. Using two of the cords, fold 7 feet (2 m) into one of the ends of the rope (this shorter side will be the filler cord) and attach both cords on the outside of the outer panel, using a lark's head knot, so the filler cords are on the inside, framed by the working cords on the outside. Repeat this on both sides of the backdrop.

30. Working on the left side, using the cords you just added, tie 159 right-facing half knot sinnets. On the right side, tie 159 left-facing half knot sinnets. These half knot sinnets should be approximately 56 inches (142 cm) long. Bundle the working cords (page 158) to make tying with the long cords more manageable.

31. Cut 2 pieces of ³⁄₁₆-inch (5-mm) three-strand rope at 3 feet (91.5 cm). On both sides, under the half knot sinnets you just tied, tie a gathering knot that is 1⅝ inches (4 cm) wide by leaving a tail of 37 inches (94 cm) hanging down with the other cords so it becomes a part of the fringe and then fold over and start wrapping. Cut the cords from these half knot sinnets to 6 feet (1.8 m) long.

31

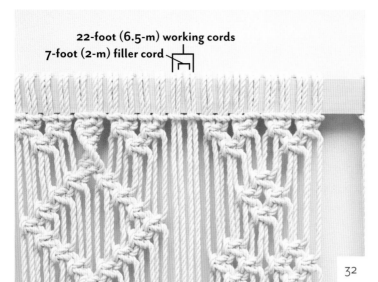

22-foot (6.5-m) working cords
7-foot (2-m) filler cord

32

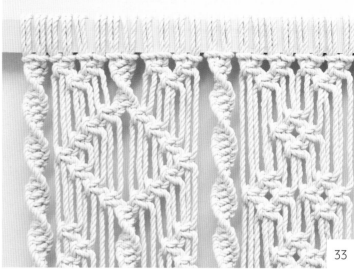

33

34

32. To make the next half knot sinnets between the outer and the inner panel, cut 4 strands of ³⁄₁₆-inch (5-mm) three-strand rope, 29 feet (9 m) long. Using two of the cords, fold 7 feet (2 m) into one of the ends of rope (this shorter side will be the filler cord) and attach both cords in the 1-inch (2.5-cm) space between the outer and the inner panels, using a lark's head knot, so the filler cords are on the inside, framed by the working cords on the outside. Repeat this on both sides of the piece.

33. Working on the left side, using the cords you just added, tie 102 right-facing half knot sinnets. On the right side, tie 102 left-facing half knot sinnets. These half knot sinnets should be approximately 34½ inches (87.5 cm) long. Bundle the working cords the same way as step 30 to make tying with the long cords more manageable.

34. Repeat step 31.

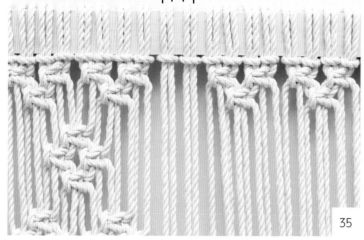

14-foot (4.5-m) working cords
7-foot (2-m) filler cord

35

36

35. To make the next half knot sinnets between the inner and center panel, cut 4 strands of ³⁄₁₆-inch (5-mm) three-strand rope, 21 feet (6.5 m) long. Using two of the cords, fold 6 feet (1.8 m) into one of the ends of rope (this shorter side will be the filler cord) and attach both cords in the 1-inch (2.5-cm) space between the inner and the center panel, using a lark's head knot, so the filler cords are on the inside, framed by the working cords on the outside. Repeat this on both sides of the piece.

36. Working on the left side, using the cords you just added, tie 73 right-facing half knot sinnets. On the right side, tie 73 left-facing half knot sinnets. These half knot sinnets should be approximately 26 inches (66 cm) long. Bundle the working cords the same way as step 30 to make tying with the long cords more manageable.

37. Cut 2 pieces of ³⁄₁₆-inch (5-mm) three-strand rope at 66 inches (167.5 cm). On both sides, under the half knot sinnets you just tied, tie a gathering knot that is 1⅝ inches (4 cm) wide, by leaving a tail of 36 inches (91.5 cm) hanging down with the other cords so it becomes a part of the fringe and then fold over and start wrapping. Cut all of the cords from these half knot sinnets to 62 inches (157.5 cm).

37

38

39

FRINGE OVERLAY

Try to use leftover or scrap rope from this project or any others to create the overlay! It saves money and is less wasteful.

38. Cut 1 strand of ³⁄₁₆-inch (5-mm) three-strand rope at 123 inches (3 m). Fold this piece in half and attach to the very middle of the wood and in between the cords, using a lark's head knot.

39. With the cord you just added, using the side of the cord, measure 28 inches (71 cm) over and attach to the very left side of the wood with a continuous lark's head knot. This will make the rope hang in a swooped manner in front of the backdrop. Tie an overhand knot with the remaining hanging cord tight to the continuous lark's head knot you just tied. The photo shows an overhand knot before it has been pulled tight. Repeat this on the right side. This is your overlay cord.

40. For this step, use your scrap rope when possible. Cut 20 pieces of ³⁄₁₆-inch (5-mm) three-strand rope at 14 inches (35.5 cm) long. Fold each cord in half and attach 10 cords using a lark's head knot on either side of the middle, working outwards, on the overlay cord.

Use a lark's head knot to attach the following cords. Cut 12 strands of ³⁄₁₆-inch (5-mm) three-strand rope at 16 inches (40.5 cm). Fold each cord in half and attach 6 cords on either side, next to the cords you just added. Cut 14 strands of ³⁄₁₆-inch (5-mm) three-strand rope at 18 inches (45.5 cm). Fold each cord in half and attach 7 cords on either side next to the cords you just added. Cut 8 strands of ³⁄₁₆-inch (5-mm) three-strand rope at 20 inches (51 cm). Fold each cord in half and attach 4 cords on either side next to the cords you just added.

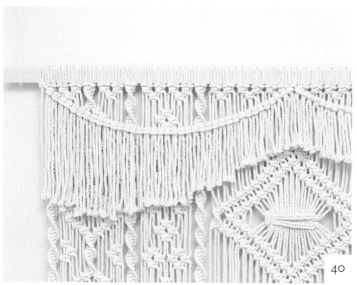

40

41

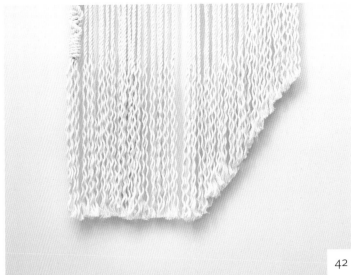

42

Cut 8 strands of ³⁄₁₆-inch (5-mm) three-strand rope at 22 inches (56 cm). Fold each cord in half and attach 4 cords on either side next to the cords you just added. Cut 8 strands of ³⁄₁₆-inch (5-mm) three-strand rope at 24 inches (61 cm). Fold each cord in half and attach 4 cords on either side next to the cords you just added.

Cut 8 strands of ³⁄₁₆-inch (5-mm) three-strand rope at 26 inches (66 cm). Fold each cord in half and attach 4 cords on either side next to the cords you just added.

41. Unravel the cords from the center panel and the fringe overlay (page 158).

42. Unravel the cords from the inner and outer panels shown in the angled pattern from the photo or to your preference.

hanging tip:

This is deceptively heavy. Make sure you hang it securely, so it does not injure anyone at an event! Use the technique shown on page 20 if you are hanging it on the wall or arch. If you are hanging it from a ceiling, simply thread rope that can bear the weight of the piece, around the wood and in between the lark's head knots, a foot or so in from the ends of the piece. My piece weighed 13⅓ pounds (6 kg), but to be safe you should always weigh your own finished piece. See page 10 for an easy way to weigh large macramé pieces. Note that if you make any adjustments to the project, it may change the weight.

PRISM CURTAIN

After I finished making each project in this book, I would pack the piece away somewhere in my home studio for future use. I did that for every single project except the Prism Curtain, which I hung in the doorway between my kitchen and living room because I loved it so much! Whether you use this piece in a doorway or as window curtains, it adds a pleasant textural element to the space. I especially love the gradient of knots that gradually fade as your eye moves down the string. A door curtain is a fun way to add some art to a room without being confined to simply hanging it on a wall. It's also nice because it can break up two spaces in a way that isn't as heavy or permanent as a door. It creates a nice transition between the rooms and gives you a whimsical sense of fun every time you walk through it! Believe it or not, my cats walk right through it without a care (they are quite used to rope around here)!

Tips: If you would like to alter the curtain's width to be larger or smaller, work in increments of 14 cords (each swoop) and follow the steps.

You can make this project twice to hang on either side of a window like traditional curtains. If you want to put it on a curtain rod, use curtain rings, like the ones suggested in the materials recommendations, and add them using the ring opening on the loops created by the overhand knot (page 134).

skill level: advanced

DIMENSIONS
32 inches (81 cm) wide (hanging as shown in photo) x 80 inches (203 cm) tall

MATERIALS AND TOOLS
About 1,807 feet (550.8 m) of ⅛-inch (3-mm) single-strand string

1 (32-inch [81-cm] or longer) wooden dowel (for temporary use only)

Slicker brush

Large-eye needle

Pliers (optional)

Curtain rings (optional)

KNOTS USED
Overhand Knot with Loop (page 134)

Lark's Head Knot (page 127)

Diagonal Alternating Square Knot (page 147)

Cluster of 3 and 4 Square Knots (page 148)

Half Knot Sinnet (left- and right-facing) (page 141)

Double Half Hitch (page 132)

Double Half Hitch Diamond (page 155)

Diamond of Double Half Hitches (page 156)

Square Knot with Multiple Filler and Working Cords (page 131)

Barrel Knot (page 136)

Rya Knot (Tassel) (page 139)

1. Cut 1 piece of ⅛-inch (3-mm) single-strand string, 80 inches (2 m) long. We'll work a little differently to start this project, creating loops with the string through which you will then thread the dowel. Measure from the end of the string to leave a 6-inch (15-cm) tail. Then, using only 5 inches (13 cm) of string, tie an overhand knot with a loop (page 134), creating a ½-inch (1.3-cm) loop. Measuring 7½ inches (19 cm) over from the last overhand knot with a loop, tie another overhand knot the same way with the same amount of string. Do this 4 more times. This will leave you with an approximately 6-inch (15-cm) tail at the end of the string. Thread the dowel through the loops created by the looped overhand knots. Space the knots 6½ inches (16.5 cm) apart. See the next step's photo for spacing reference.

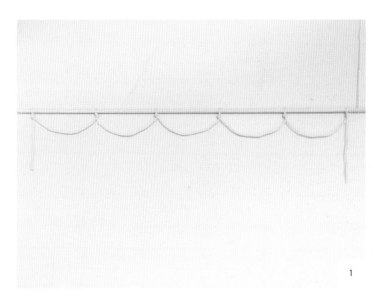

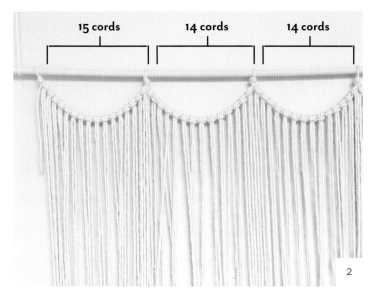

15 cords   14 cords   14 cords

3

4

5

2. Cut 72 pieces of ⅛-inch (3-mm) single-strand string, 25 feet (7.5 m) long. Fold each piece in half and attach 15 strands, using a lark's head knot, onto the far left and far right swooped sections. Attach the remaining cords by folding them in half and using a lark's head knot, 14 strands to each of the middle swooped sections. This is important or it will throw off the pattern.

3. Starting on the left side under the overhand knot with a loop, tie 7 diagonal alternating square knots angling down and to the right, leaving a ¼-inch (6-mm) space from the lark's head knots above and leaving no space between each square knot. Do your best to follow the angle of the swoop. Below the next overhand knot with a loop, tie 7 diagonal alternating square knots angling down and to the left, leaving the same amount of space. Tie one last alternating square knot, joining both rows together. Do this 4 more times across the full length of the curtain.

4. Under the overhand knot and upside-down V created by the square knots from the last step, tie a cluster of 4 square knots (page 148) in the middle of the 4 upside-down Vs, 1½ inches (4 cm) down from the last row. Tie a cluster of 3 square knots (page 148) on both sides of the curtain at the same height.

5. Starting under the lowest square knot on the left from step 3, tie 1 row of 6 diagonal alternating square knots angling down and to the left, leaving no space between each knot. Starting under the first square knot of the row you just tied, tie another row of 6 diagonal alternating square knots angling down and to the right, leaving no space between each knot. Continue this 4 more times, under the bottom square knots from step 3.

6

7

8

6. Starting on the far left of the curtain, at the bottom of the last row of square knots, tie 29 right-facing half knot sinnets so that the sinnet measures 5¼ inches (13 cm) long, tight to the knots above. This will connect the two rows of square knots. Working left to right, in the same spot, tie 29 half knots in each spot to create 6 half knot sinnets, making sure to tie each sinnet alternating between each other—left-facing, right-facing, left-facing—until you reach the end of the curtain.

7. Staring back on the left side of the curtain, using the middle two cords in between the half knot sinnets, measuring 6 inches (15 cm) down from the dowel, tie a row of 6 diagonal double half hitches angling down and to the right, matching the angle of the square knots above. Using the working cord from the first double half hitch as a filler cord, tie 5 double half hitches around this filler cord angling down and to the left, matching the angle as the row of square knots above. Do this 4 more times in between each of the half knot sinnets.

8. Starting back on the left side of the curtain, under the right row of double half hitches, skip over 2 cords and tie another row of 5 diagonal double half hitches tight to the row above. This will offset the rows by 2 cords. On the left side, tie another row of 5 double half hitches, mirroring the right side so it is also offset by 2 cords. Do this 4 more times under the other double half hitch rows from the previous step.

9. Starting back on the left side of the curtain, under the last right row of double half hitches, skip over 2 cords, tie another row of 5 double half hitches tight to the row above, offsetting the rows by 2 cords. On the left side, tie another row of 5 double half hitches, mirroring the right side so it is also offset by 2 cords. Do this 4 more times under the other double half hitches from the previous step.

9

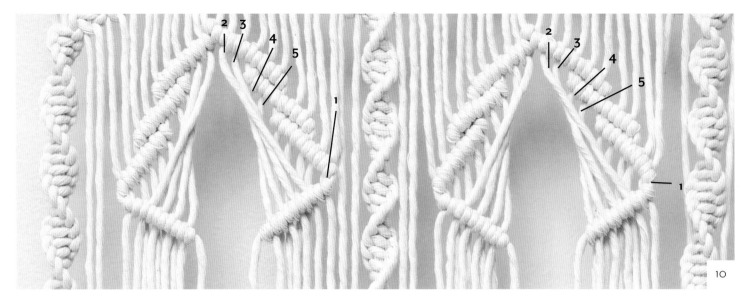

10

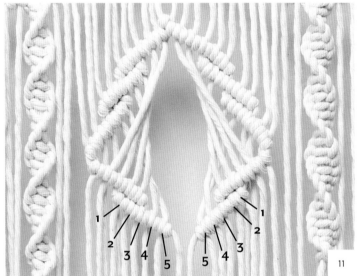

11

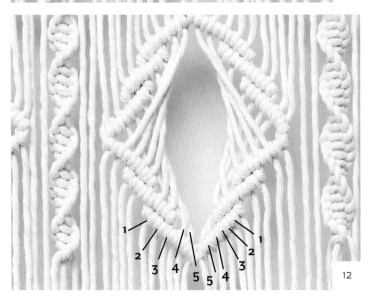

10. Starting back on the left side of the curtain, on the right side of the half diamond, using the filler cord from the previous step's row of double half hitches, angle the cord leftward at a 90-degree angle and use the cords to tie 5 double half hitches in the order stated in the photo (1, 2, 3, etc.). Do the same and mirror it on the left side of the diamond. Repeat these steps 4 more times on each of the other diamonds. Take extra time to make sure you are taking the right cords in this step and the next 3 steps.

11. Starting back on the left side of the curtain, skipping over 2 cords, tie another row of 5 double half hitches under the previous row using the corresponding cords from the photo to continue the pattern. For your first 3 knots, you will use the cords coming from the double half hitch directly above, and 2 cords from above. Do the same and mirror it on the left side of the diamond. Repeat these steps 4 more times on each of the other diamonds. Use the order referenced in the photo, to help clarify.

12. Starting back on the left side of the curtain, skipping over 2 cords, tie another row of 5 double half hitches under the previous row using the corresponding cords to continue the pattern. For your first 3 knots, you will use the cords coming from the double half hitch directly above, and 2 cords from above. Do this on the left side of the diamond and join it to the right side using the right filler cord to tie a double half hitch around the left side's filler cord. Continue this 4 more times under the rest of the double half hitches from the previous step. Use the order referenced in the photo, to help clarify.

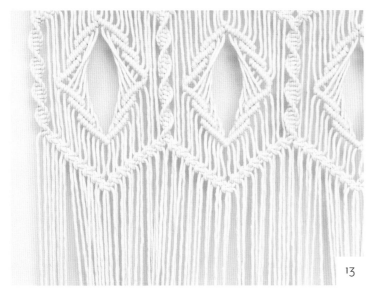

13

14

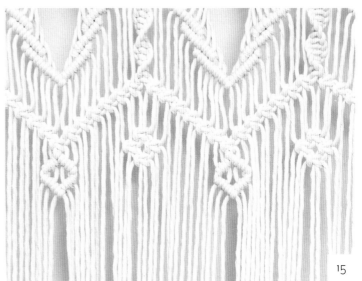

15

13. Starting back on the left side of the curtain, under the half knot sinnets, tie a row of 6 diagonal alternating square knots angling down and toward the right. Under the next half knot sinnet, tie a row of 7 diagonal alternating square knots, angling down and towards the left. The last square knot will join the row of square knots from the previous step. Repeat this 4 more times under each of the other diamonds.

14. Starting back on the left side of the curtain, measuring 1½ inches (4 cm) down from the last row, tie a cluster of 4 square knots under the upside-down V of alternating square knots. Repeat this 4 times across the curtain. Tie a cluster of 3 square knots at the same height on either edge of the curtain.

15. Starting back on the left side of the curtain, under the last square knot from step 13 (under the V of alternating square knots), tie a double half hitch diamond (page 155) using a total of 6 cords. Tie 4 more diamonds under the 4 other Vs.

16. Starting back on the left side of the curtain, under the double half hitch diamond you tied from the previous step, tie another double half hitch diamond, using a total of 10 cords, with a square knot tied with 4 filler cords and 1 working cord for each side, in the middle of the diamond. When starting this diamond, continue tying with the same filler cord used in the first diamond in the previous step; this way the diamonds are connected. Do this 4 more times across the curtain.

16

17

18

19

20

17. Starting back on the left side of the curtain, tie another double half hitch diamond, using a total of 6 cords under the diamond from the previous step. Keep the diamond connected by continuing to tie with the same filler cord used in the last diamond in the previous step.

18. Starting just under the full last row of alternating square knots, tie multiple barrel knots in different placements throughout the curtain so they don't sit right next to each other. Create a gradient of barrel knots by tying a higher density of knots at the top, and then gradually tie fewer and spread out the barrel knots as you work your way down the curtain. Use your intuition on the number and placement of the knots depending on what feels right. The exact placement doesn't matter, just the effect it gives of a gradient from top to bottom.

19. Trim all the cords to 80 inches (2 m) from the dowel (or your door/window height). Place the excess cut-off strands to the side for the next step.

20. Using the scrap rope you cut from the previous step, find 10 pieces of rope that are 11 inches (28 cm) or longer—if longer, cut them to 11 inches (28 cm). Take two cords and attach them by tying a rya knot (tassel) (page 139) to the middle of the bottom diamond tied in step 17. Tie 4 more rya knots to the remaining 4 diamonds.

21

22

21. Brush out the 5 tassels with a slicker brush (page 159). Trim the tassels so they are all the same length at 4¾ inches (12 cm) or your desired length.

22. Sew the 6-inch (15-cm) tails from step 1 into the backs of 4 of the lark's head knots, using a large-eye needle. Now you can hang it in a doorway with nails, hooking the loops over the nails, or as curtains on either side of a window.

   Note that my piece weighed 1⅘ pounds (1 kg), but to be safe you should always weigh your own finished piece. See page 10 for an easy way to weigh large macramé pieces. Note that if you make any adjustments to the project, it may change the weight.

optional for curtain rings:

If you want to use this as a window curtain, add these curtain rod rings to the loops created by the overhand knot. You may need pliers if the rings are stiff to move. See the resource list for buying options (page 160).

VENICE BACKDROP

This project is a true showstopper for a wedding, for a baby or bridal shower backdrop or as décor for any other type of event. The directional pattern draws your eye toward the center and the piece's symmetry makes it really stand out. The straight lines mixed with the twisting knots create a striking design. This would also make an amazing oversized wall hanging for a large space with high ceilings. You can take this backdrop to the next level by decorating the top of it with some greenery like pampas grass, Italian ruscus, eucalyptus or florals.

Tips : Make sure you line the knots up on each panel with the knots on your panel beside it. I will tell you the heights to tie the knots, but it's more important that your own knots align panel to panel, so keep this in mind while you work and start the next panel. You can push up or pull down on the sinnets to lengthen or shorten them slightly.

skill level: advanced

DIMENSIONS
58 inches (147 cm) wide (not including wood) x 6 feet (1.8 m) tall

MATERIALS AND TOOLS
About 2,371.5 feet (722.8 m) of ³⁄₁₆-inch (5-mm) single-strand cotton string

1 wood piece 6 feet (1.8 m) long x ¾ inch (2 cm) wide x 2 inches (5 cm) thick (I used oak)

Rope/hooks or screws for hanging

KNOTS USED
Lark's Head Knot (page 127)

Half Knot Sinnet (page 141)

Square Knot (page 130)

Alternating Square Knot (page 143)

Double Half Hitches (page 132)

Diagonal Alternating Square Knot (page 147)

Barrel Knot (page 136)

Gathering Knot (page 138)

OUTER PANELS

1. To create the two outer panels, cut 32 pieces of ³⁄₁₆-inch (5-mm) single-strand string at 22 feet (6.5 m). Fold each cord in half and attach 16 cords with a lark's head knot, 6 inches (15 cm) in from either end of the wood.

left outer panel

2. Working left to right, skip the first 2 cords and tie 11 left-facing half knots to create a 3¼-inch (8-cm) half knot sinnet. Skip the next two cords, and tie 15 left-facing half knots to create a 5-inch (13-cm) half knot sinnet. Skip the next two cords, and tie 22 left-facing half knots to create a 6¾-inch (17-cm) half knot sinnet. Tie each of these sinnets tight to the wood.

1

2

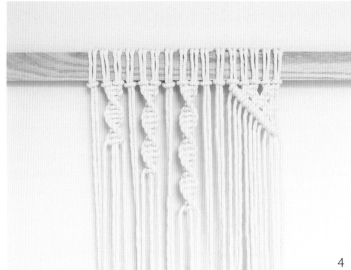

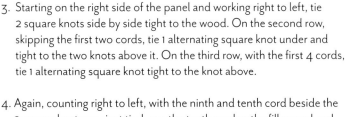

3. Starting on the right side of the panel and working right to left, tie 2 square knots side by side tight to the wood. On the second row, skipping the first two cords, tie 1 alternating square knot under and tight to the two knots above it. On the third row, with the first 4 cords, tie 1 alternating square knot tight to the knot above.

4. Again, counting right to left, with the ninth and tenth cord beside the 2 square knots you just tied, use the tenth cord as the filler cord and angle it to the right below the square knots you tied in the previous step. Tie 9 diagonal double half hitches tight to the knots above. Tie the first knot tight to the wood.

5. Again, counting right to left, tie a square knot with the eleventh, twelfth, thirteenth and fourteenth cords tight to the wood. Tie 5 alternating square knots angling down and to the right, tight to each other and the row of knots above.

6. Now, working from left to right, skipping two cords from the last half knot sinnet you tied in step 2 and under the diagonal row of alternating square knots, tie 24 left-facing half knots to create a 7-inch (17.5-cm) half knot sinnet. Repeat this one more time to tie another half knot sinnet two cords over.

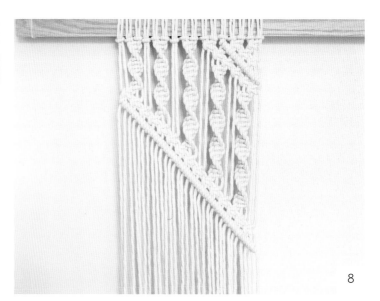

7

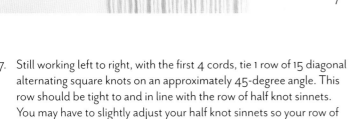

8

9

7. Still working left to right, with the first 4 cords, tie 1 row of 15 diagonal alternating square knots on an approximately 45-degree angle. This row should be tight to and in line with the row of half knot sinnets. You may have to slightly adjust your half knot sinnets so your row of alternating square knots looks even.

8. Still working left to right, using the first cord as the filler cord, holding it diagonally down and to the right, tie 31 double half hitches with each cord, directly below and following the same angle as the row above.

9. Still working left to right, using the first 4 cords, tie 2 rows of 15 diagonal alternating square knots (15 knots per row) tight to and matching the angle of the knots above it.

10. Still working left to right, using the first 4 cords 7¼ inches (18.5 cm) down from the previous row above, tie 1 row of 15 diagonal alternating square knots, matching the angle of the knots above it. Keep checking your spacing by measuring every knot or so.

10

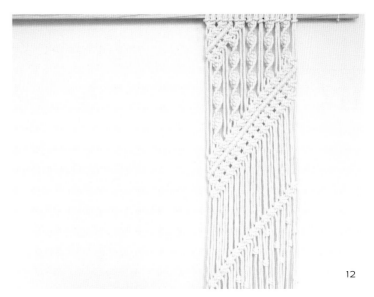

11. Tie a gradient of barrel knots throughout the panel, with a larger concentration of knots at the top and gradually lessening as you work your way down the cords. After tying all of your barrel knots, cut all of the cords to 6 feet (1.8 m).

right outer panel

12. Repeat steps 2 to 11 on the outer right panel, but mirror the steps and make sure to tie right-facing half knot sinnets so both turn toward the middle.

INNER PANELS

13. To create the two inner panels, cut 32 pieces of ³⁄₁₆-inch (5-mm) single-strand string at 22 feet (6.5 m). Fold each cord in half and attach 16 cords with a lark's head knot, 1¼ inches (3 cm) over from the outer panels. This 1¼-inch (3-cm) space leaves room for the half knot sinnets to be added in between the panels in a later step.

left inner panel

For all of these steps, work from left to right on the panel.

14. Measuring down 2 inches (5 cm) from the bottom of the wood, tie 2 rows of 15 diagonal alternating square knots (15 knots per row) angling down at an approximately 45-degree angle and to the right. Try to match the angle of the alternating square knots at the top of the outer panel.

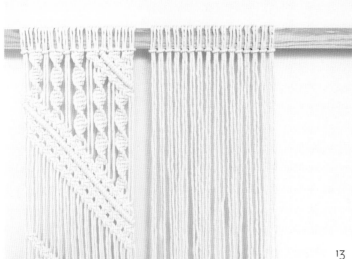

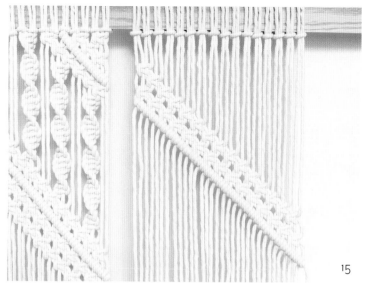

15

16

17

15. Using the first cord as the filler cord, holding it diagonally down and to the right, tie 31 double half hitches with each cord, directly below and following the same angle as the row above.

16. Tie 1 row of 15 diagonal alternating square knots, angling down and to the right, tight to the row above.

17. Tying all knots tight to the row above it, skip the first 2 cords and using the next 4 cords, tie 24 left-facing half knots to create a 7-inch (17.5-cm) half knot sinnet. Repeat this step 4 more times, so you have a total of 5 half knot sinnets.

18. Using the first 4 cords, tie 1 row of 15 diagonal alternating square knots on an approximately 45-degree angle. This row should be tight to and in line with the row of half knot sinnets. You may have to slightly adjust your half knot sinnets so your row of alternating square knots looks even.

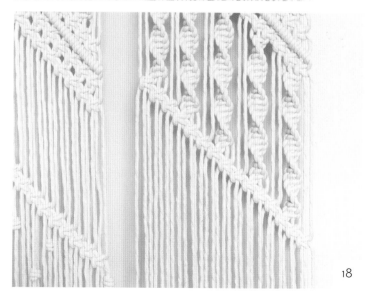

18

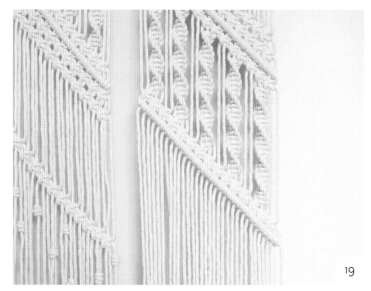

19

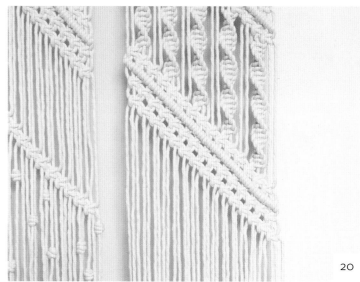

20

21

19. Using the first cord as the filler cord, holding it diagonally down and to the right, tie 31 double half hitches with each cord, directly below and following the same angle as the row above.

20. Tie 2 rows of 15 diagonal alternating square knots (15 knots per row) angling down and to the right, tight to and matching the angle of the knots above it.

21. Using the first 4 cords, measuring 7¼ inches (18.5 cm) down from the previous row's knots, tie 1 row of 15 diagonal alternating square knots, matching the angle of the knots above it. Keep checking your spacing by measuring every knot or so.

22. Tie a gradient of barrel knots throughout the panel, with a larger concentration of knots at the top and gradually lessening as you work your way down the cords. Tie somewhat fewer knots at the top of the gradient then you did for the outer panel. After tying all of your barrel knots, cut all of the cords to 6 feet (1.8 m).

22

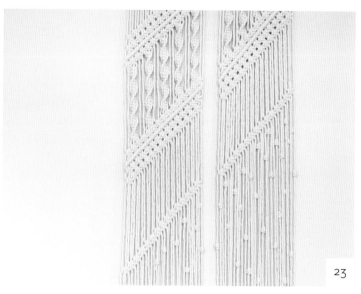

23

24

right inner panel

23. Repeat steps 14 to 22 on the inner right panel, but mirror the steps and make sure to tie right-facing half knot sinnets so both turn toward the middle.

CENTER PANELS

24. To create the center panels, cut 32 strands of ³⁄₁₆-inch (5-mm) single-strand string at 27 feet (8 m). Fold each cord in half and attach 16 cords with a lark's head knot, 1¼ inches (3 cm) in from the inner panels. This 1¼-inch (3-cm) space leaves room for you to add the half knot sinnets in between the panels in a later step. There should be another 1¼-inch (3-cm) space in the very middle between both center panels; you can slightly shift the panels on the wood if you don't have enough space in the middle.

left center panel

25. Working right to left, with the first 12 cords, tie 3 square knots side by side, tight to the wood. For the second row, skip the first 2 cords and tie 2 alternating square knots tight to the row above. For the third row, with the first 8 cords, tie 2 alternating square knots tight to the row above. For the fourth row, skip the first 2 cords and tie 1 alternating square knot tight to the row above. For the fifth row, tie one square knot with the first 4 cords, tight to the knots above.

25

26

27

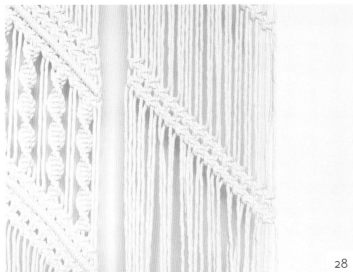

28

26. Working right to left, using the thirteenth and fourteenth cords beside the 3 square knots you just tied, and using the fourteenth cord as the filler cord, angle it to the right below the square knots you tied in the previous step. Tie 13 diagonal double half hitches tight to the knots above and tie the first knot tight to the wood.

27. Working left to right, using the first 4 cords, tie 1 row of 15 diagonal alternating square knots at an approximately 45-degree angle and matching the angle of the knots above it, and tie the first knot tight to the piece of wood. The last square knot on the far-right side measures 4½ inches (11.5 cm) down from the double half hitch row above it.

28. Working left to right, using the first 4 cords and measuring 9½ inches (24 cm) down from the previous row above, tie 2 rows of 15 diagonal alternating square knots (15 knots per row), matching the angle of the knots above it. Keep checking your spacing by measuring every few knots.

29. Working left to right, using the first cord as the filler cord, holding it diagonally down and to the right, tie 31 double half hitches with every cord directly below and following the same angle as the row above.

29

30

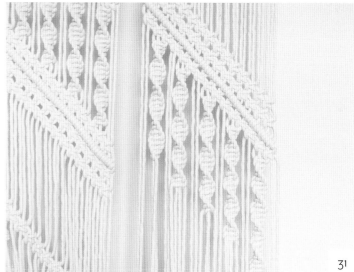

31

30. Working left to right, tie 1 row of 15 diagonal alternating square knots angling down and to the right, tight to the row above.

31. Working left to right, tying all knots tight to the row above, skip the first 2 cords and tie 24 right-facing half knots to create a 7-inch (17.5-cm) half knot sinnet. Repeat this step 4 more times, so you have a total of 5 half knot sinnets.

32. Working left to right, with the first 4 cords, tie 1 row of 15 diagonal alternating square knots on an approximately 45-degree angle. This row should be tight and in line with the row of half knot sinnets. You may have to slightly adjust your half knot sinnets so your row of alternating square knots looks even.

33. Working left to right and using the first cord as the filler cord, holding it diagonally down and to the right, tie 31 double half hitch knots directly below and following the same angle as the row above with each cord.

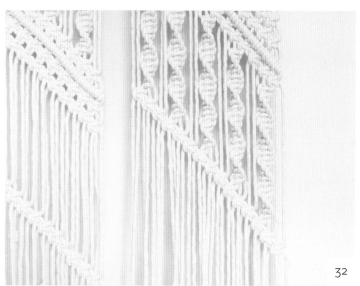

32

33

34

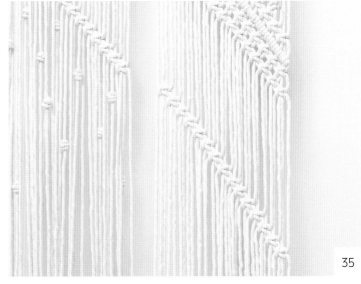

35

36

34. Working left to right, tie 2 rows of 15 diagonal alternating square knots (15 knots per row) angling down and to the right, tight to and matching the angle of the knots above.

35. Working left to right, using the first 4 cords, measuring 7¼ inches (18.5 cm) down from the previous row above, tie 1 row of 15 diagonal alternating square knots, matching the angle of the knots above it. Keep checking your spacing by measuring every knot or so.

36. Tie a gradient of barrel knots throughout the panel, with a larger concentration of knots at the top and gradually lessening as you work your way down the cords. Tie somewhat fewer knots at the top of the gradient then you did for the inner panel. After tying all of your barrel knots, cut all of the cords to 6 feet (1.8 m).

right center panel

37. Repeat steps 25 to 36 on the center right panel, but mirror the steps and make sure to tie right-facing half knot sinnets so both turn toward the middle.

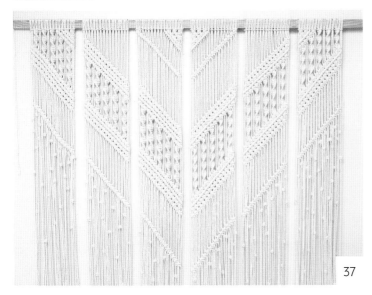

37

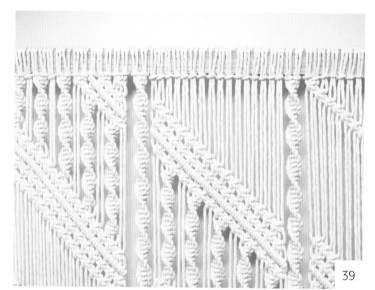

36⅛-inch (91.7-cm) working cords
82½-inch (2-m) filler cord

38

39

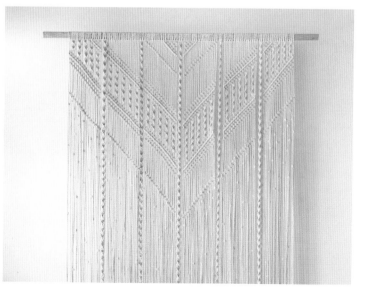

40

MAKING THE HALF KNOT SINNET TASSELS

38. Cut 10 pieces of ³⁄₁₆-inch (5-mm) single-strand string at 43 feet (13 m). Fold each cord 82½ inches (2 m) in from the end (this shorter side will be the filler cord). Attach two cords in the 1-inch (2.5-cm) space between each of the panels, using a lark's head knot so the filler cords are on the inside, framed by the working cords on the outside. Do this in each of the five 1¼-inch (3-cm) spaces.

39. Tie 228 half knot sinnets on each tassel, so each one is 65 inches (165 cm) long, measuring from the bottom of the wood. Make the 3 tassels on the left all right-facing, and the 2 tassels on the right left-facing.

40. Cut 5 pieces of ³⁄₁₆-inch (5-mm) single-strand string at 30 inches (76 cm). Fold the cord over at 13 inches (33 cm) and tie a 1¼-inch (3-cm)-wide gathering knot around the last half knot on each sinnet. Trim all of the fringe on each tassel to 6 feet (1.8 m) long, measuring from the bottom of the wood.

hanging tips:

This is deceptively heavy; make sure you hang it securely so it does not injure anyone at an event! Use the technique shown on page 20 if you are hanging it on the wall or arch. If you are hanging it from a ceiling, simply thread rope that can bear the weight of the piece around the wood and in between the lark's head knots, a foot or so in from the ends of the piece.

My piece weighed 14½ pounds (6.5 kg), but to be safe you should always weigh your own finished piece. See page 10 for an easy way to weigh large macramé pieces. Note that if you make any adjustments to the project, it may change the weight.

GOING BEYOND
THE PROJECTS AND
MY APPROACH

Macramé really is the perfect art form for those who love making unique designs because there are so many different knots, patterns and combinations available for use. I always warn people that it can be addicting, because once you fall in love with it, you'll have endless ideas and opportunities. Just like my last book, I designed each of the projects to help you practice different techniques in order to ultimately have the skills to create your own unique designs. I hope some of these concepts inspire you and help you feel confident in creating your own designs!

I get a lot of questions about how to get started tackling large-scale macramé, and although I'm always still learning, I wanted to share more about my approach and some general tips that I've learned that will hopefully help you along the way.

Sometimes working large means thinking creatively and problem-solving. Don't be afraid to think outside of the box and come up with a unique approach! In the paragraphs below, I've shared some tips that can be helpful when working on your own designs or adapting the designs I've shared in this book.

START WITH A PLAN AND DRAWING

I find it incredibly helpful to make a drawing of the piece as a first step. This helps me visualize the project in its entirety and have a road map for where I'm heading. I actually make a rough sketch of each individual knot in order to work out most of the pattern in advance.

Of course, things may change a little when you actually begin working with the rope because of things like the number of cords, the scale, weight, etc. But drawing the piece is always a great starting point for me. This is where I also keep track of all the rope lengths that I need for each project. This is especially helpful when I want to recreate a similar pattern later, as it gives me a starting point for the length of rope needed.

TEST WITH A SAMPLE

Depending on the piece, it can be helpful to make a small sample to work out the design before fully committing and cutting all of the rope. You want to be sure to save yourself having to add more rope if you run out (see page 159 to learn how to add rope). This can also be a helpful way to figure out what lengths of rope you'll need if you're completely unsure. Test it with just 4 to 8 cords in the pattern you're planning.

GET CREATIVE

Changing the spacing of your knots will alter the look of any project or pattern—such as tying the rows very close together versus leaving space between them. Try adjusting the amount of space you leave between rows and knots to create variations in your designs.

When you're working on large-scale pieces, consider the intricacy of the final design. When you take a step back and look at your piece from afar, it might look more complex then when you're working right in front of it. It's easy to overcomplicate the pattern of a large-scale piece, which can end up looking too busy when you take a few steps back. Remember that negative (blank) space is just as important as positive space (knots and patterns) in macramé, and this is amplified even more in bigger designs. For example, the Annalise Backdrop pattern (page 89) seems simple, but when you step back and look at it, it has an intricate feel.

A different diameter or type of rope can also change what a piece looks like. If you use a larger rope, the piece will look bulkier and will end up being larger. Using a smaller rope does the opposite and can mean more time spent on the project. The Trellis Room Divider (page 85) really shows what an open pattern in large rope looks like, compared with the fine cord in the Prism Curtain (page 105).

Another way to alter the design of large-scale macramé is by adding layers to create depth. The Riviere Headboard (page 27) and the Annalise Backdrop (page 89) are great examples of this. The layers add depth to the piece and help make them more visually interesting. You can really get creative with the angles and numbers of layers throughout a piece.

I sincerely hope that I've helped inspire you to create your own statement macramé pieces. Don't be afraid to experiment and make mistakes, because that's how you'll get better!

KNOTS AND PATTERNS GUIDE

One of my favorite things about macramé is the wide variety of different knots available. The following Knots and Patterns Guide contains instructions for all of the specific knots used in the book.

In addition to step-by-step instructions for each knot, I've shared information about why I tie some knots in specific ways. There are also some helpful tricks for tying certain knots when you're working with long lengths of rope, which can end up saving you a lot of time.

The great thing about macramé is that it is easy enough to undo any knot you tie, and if you make a mistake, it's not irreversible. If you find that you've made a mistake far back in your work, you can do one of two things. You can simply leave it and learn for next time, because most likely you will be the only one who notices it. Or if you're like me, and it's going to drive you crazy, you can undo it. Unfortunately, you will have to undo all the knots that were made after the mistake and then continue the pattern from that point. To avoid this, keep checking your work as you go.

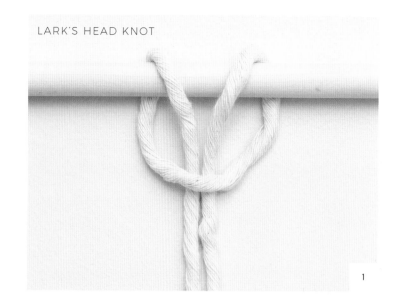

1

2

knots
LARK'S HEAD KNOT

Commonly used to attach your rope to another piece of rope, dowel or ring.

1. Begin by folding your cord in half. Place the loop over the mounting cord or dowel, carry the loop around back and bring the two ends through the loop.

2. Pull tight.

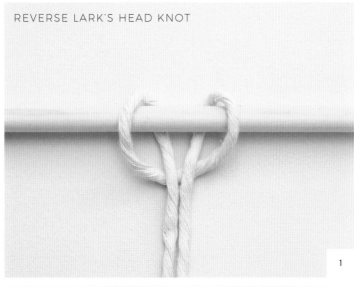

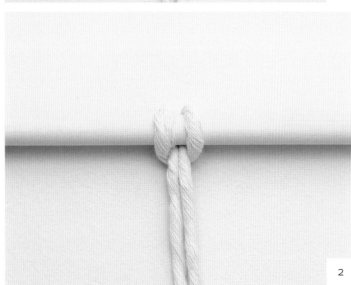

REVERSE LARK'S HEAD KNOT

1. Fold the cord in half. Place the loop under the mounting cord or dowel, carry the loop around to the front and bring the two ends through the loop.

2. Pull tight.

Tip for working large scale:

Form the knot in your hand first and then slide onto the dowel, branch or rope into position and tighten (reference the photo on the right).

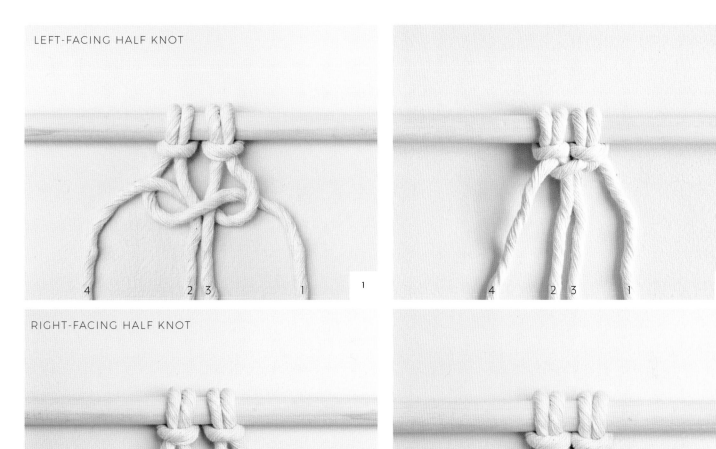

HALF KNOT

This simple knot is used to create a square knot; it is rarely used on its own because it can come undone easily.

LEFT-FACING

1. Begin the half knot by bringing cord 1 over the fillers (cords 2 and 3) and under cord 4. Cord 4 goes under the fillers and up through cords 1 and 2.

2. Pull tight.

RIGHT-FACING

1. Begin the half knot by bringing cord 4 over the fillers (cords 2 and 3) and under cord 1. Cord 1 goes under the fillers and up through cords 4 and 3.

2. Pull tight.

LEFT-FACING SQUARE KNOT

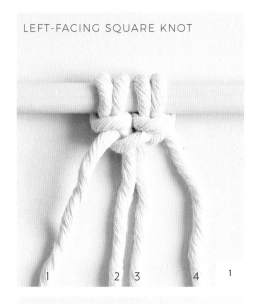
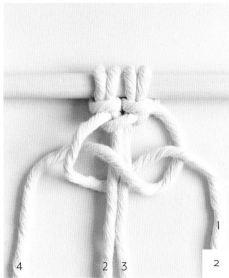

RIGHT-FACING SQUARE KNOT

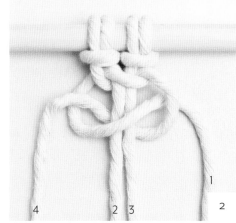
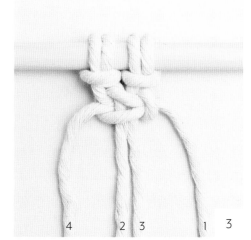

SQUARE KNOT

This is one of the most versatile and commonly used knots in macramé. I always tie left-facing square knots throughout a piece to keep it consistent, though you can also tie all right-facing knots.

LEFT-FACING

1. Start by making a left-facing half knot (page 129).

2. Place cord 4 over fillers and under cord 1. Cord 1 goes under fillers and up through cords 3 and 4.

3. Pull tight.

RIGHT-FACING

1. Start by making a right-facing half knot (page 129).

2. Place cord 1 over fillers and under cord 4. Cord 4 goes under fillers and up through cords 1 and 2.

3. Pull tight.

SQUARE KNOT WITH MULTIPLE FILLER CORDS

Changing the number of cords you tie a knot with, or around, greatly impacts the overall look of the knot. This makes a great accent knot that you can incorporate into your work.

1. Repeat all of the steps from either the left-facing or the right-facing square knot, but increase the number of filler cords to more than the regular 2 cords. Pull relatively tight, but make sure the cords don't overlap. Situate them so that they lie flat, side by side next to each other.

SQUARE KNOT WITH MULTIPLE FILLER CORDS AND MULTIPLE WORKING CORDS

This also makes a great accent knot to use in your work.

1. Repeat all of the steps from either the left-facing or the right-facing square knot, but increase the number of working cords from the usual one on each side and increase the filler cords to more than the regular 2 cords and tie around 2 or more filler cords. Pull relatively tight, making sure the cords don't overlap but instead lie flat, side by side next to each other.

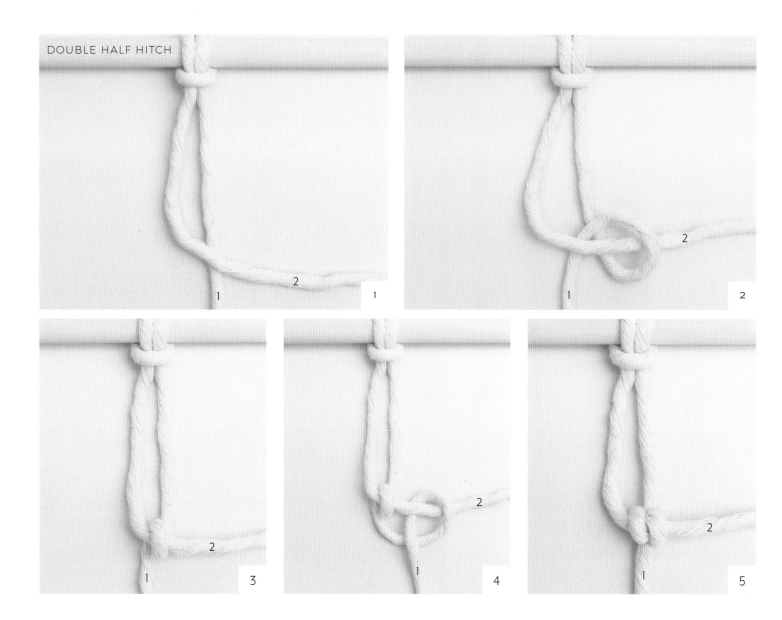

DOUBLE HALF HITCH (A.K.A. CLOVE HITCH)

This is very versatile for creating linear elements in your work.

1. Take working cord 1 and put it behind the filler cord 2 that is horizontal or diagonal to your other cords.

2. Take cord 1 and pull it up and over to the left of itself, making a clockwise loop around your filler cord.

3. Pull tight. This is one half hitch.

4. Repeat steps 1 to 3 with the same cord 1 to tie a double half hitch. This second knot is what secures the knot. Position the knots right next to each other.

5. Pull tight.

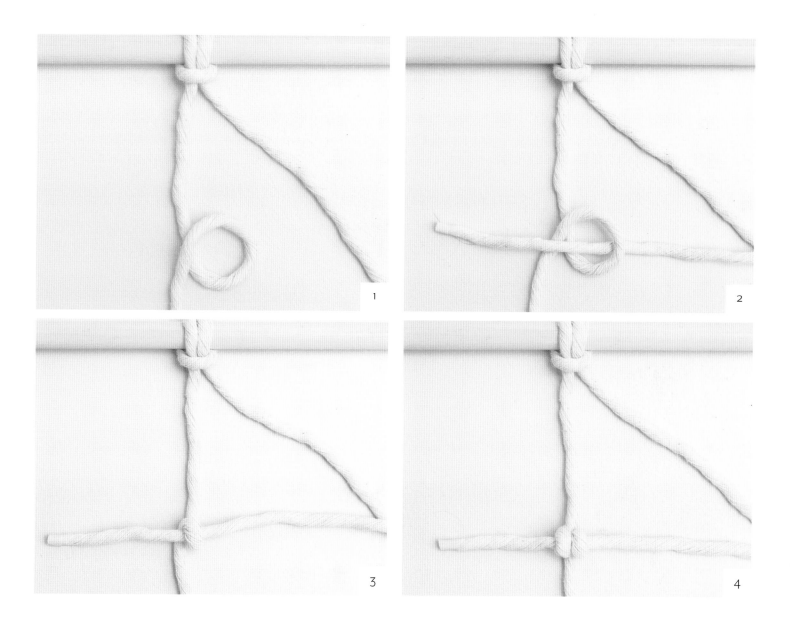

Tip for working large scale:

Try tying the double half hitch this way when your cords are very long. This saves pulling each cord through like the original technique on page 132.

1. Loop your working cord around itself counterclockwise.

2. Pull your filler cord through this loop from left to right or whatever direction row you are tying.

3. Pull tight.

4. Repeat steps 1 to 3 again with the same working cord to create a double half hitch.

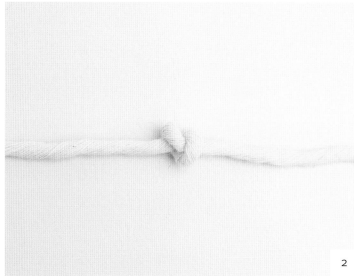

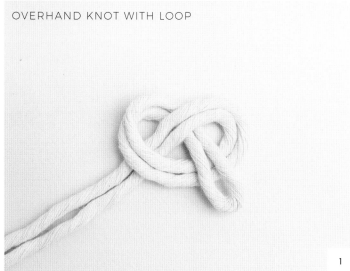

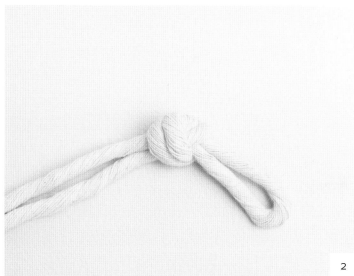

OVERHAND KNOT

This knot can be tied with multiple cords or a single cord.

1. Pass the end of the cord around itself and through the loop it forms.

2. Pull tight.

OVERHAND KNOT WITH LOOP

This knot can be tied with multiple cords or a single cord.

1. Fold the rope over on itself and pass the folded end of the cord around itself and through the loop it forms.

2. Pull tight.

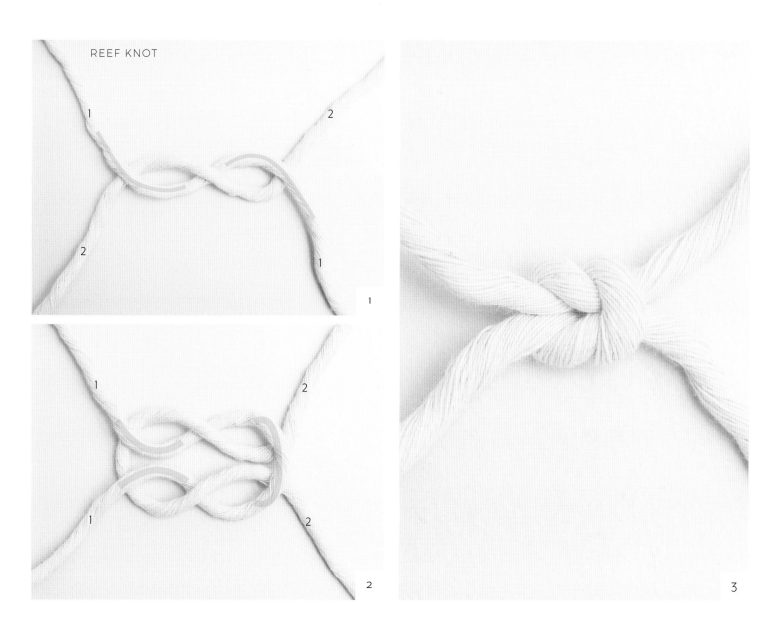

REEF KNOT (A.K.A. SQUARE KNOT)

This is one of the most common knots; you use it to tie your shoes! Not to be confused with the other square knot.

1. Using 2 cords, take cord 1 and cross it over cord 2, and then under and over cord 2.

2. Cross cord 1 over and under cord 2, then up and through the loop created by cord 2.

3. Pull tight.

1

2

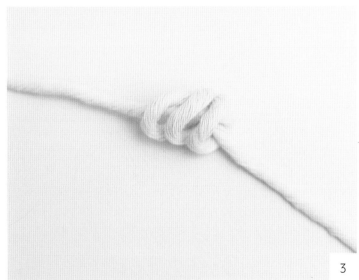

3

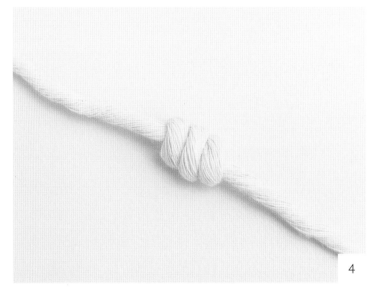

4

BARREL KNOT (A.K.A. COIL KNOT)

I love that this knot can be tied with just one cord. This decorative knot can resemble a bead on a cord and makes a perfect accent knot. It can also be helpful to keep your cords from fraying when tied near the end.

1. Using a single cord lying parallel to your finger, wrap the end loosely around your finger once.

2. Working back up and around the rope against your finger, wrap it loosely around your finger two times.

3. Carefully slide it off your finger and with the same end you've been wrapping with, from the top, thread the end through the middle of all the loops and out the end.

4. Carefully pull tight from both ends.

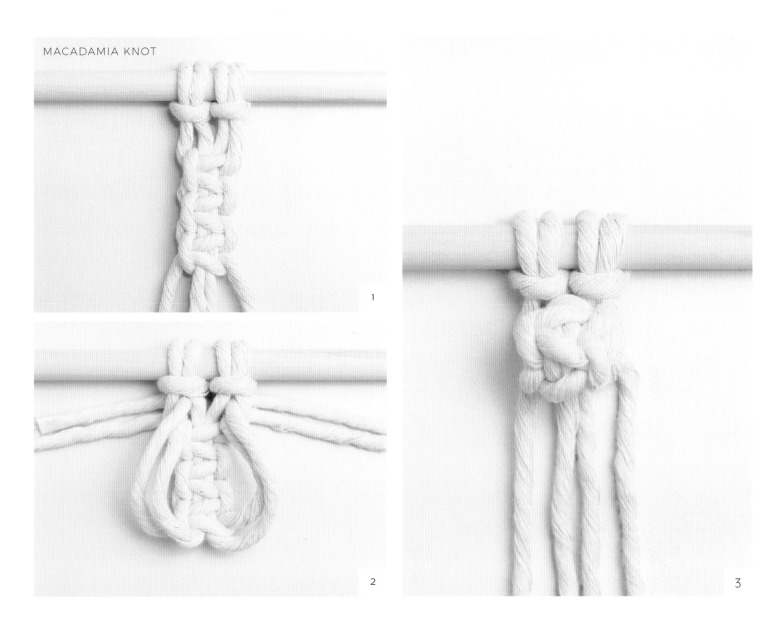

MACADAMIA KNOT

This cute knot adds a unique textural focal point as it is quite 3-D.

1. Tie 3 square knots on the same 4 cords, creating a square knot sinnet (page 140). Leave a little bit of space above the first square knot.

2. Insert the 2 filler cords and the working cords from the square knots from front to back through the holes above the top square knot.

3. Pull the cords tight so it rolls the sinnet into a ball and tie another half knot under the ball to secure it.

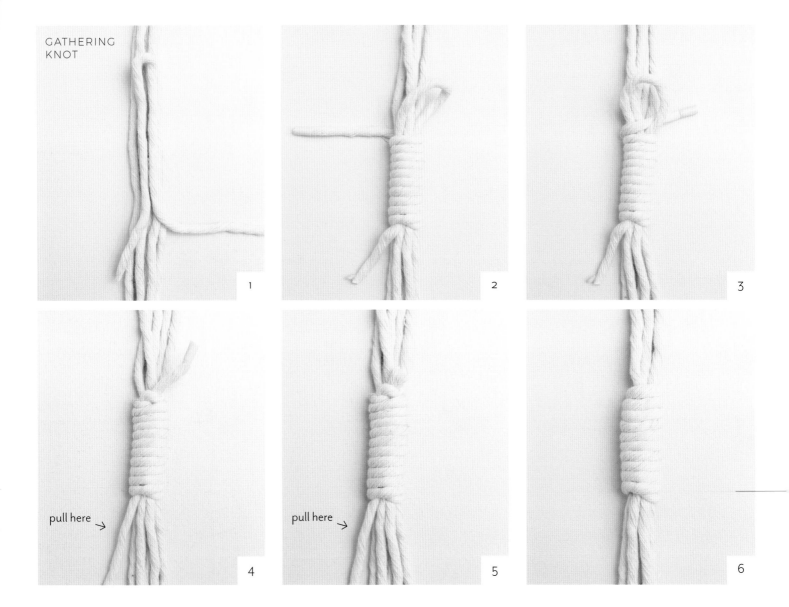

GATHERING KNOT (A.K.A. WRAPPING KNOT)

This knot is typically used to finish a plant hanger by gathering the cords together.

1. Fold a long working cord and lay it against the filler cords, leaving a 3-inch (7.5-cm) or longer tail on the bottom. The tail length changes depending on the length of gathering knot you are tying.

2. Wrap the cord upwards around all of the cords, forming what sometimes looks like a small fold at the bottom where the cord has changed direction. Holding the wrapped cord in place, continue wrapping the long end around the gathered cords and short tail. In the photo, the short tail sticks out on the left (the end is taped), and the little fold is on the right. Continue wrapping toward the loop, until you reach your desired wrapped length.

3. Pass the end of the cord you've been wrapping with through the loop.

4. Pull the loop tight by pulling the end of the cord on the bottom.

5. Trim the top cord short enough that it will hide in the gathering knot. Pull the bottom end of the cord again, so the short piece you just trimmed is pulled through the bundle and is hidden. Be careful not to pull so hard that your knot comes apart.

6. Trim the other end close to the wrapped cords, hiding it.

GATHERING KNOT FOR A TASSEL

When I tie a gathering knot for a tassel, I leave a longer tail on the cord I am pulling on in step 4 and then I unravel the longer tail so it becomes part of the fringe. You do not have to do it this way, but it is why some of the cords for gathering knots throughout the book are longer.

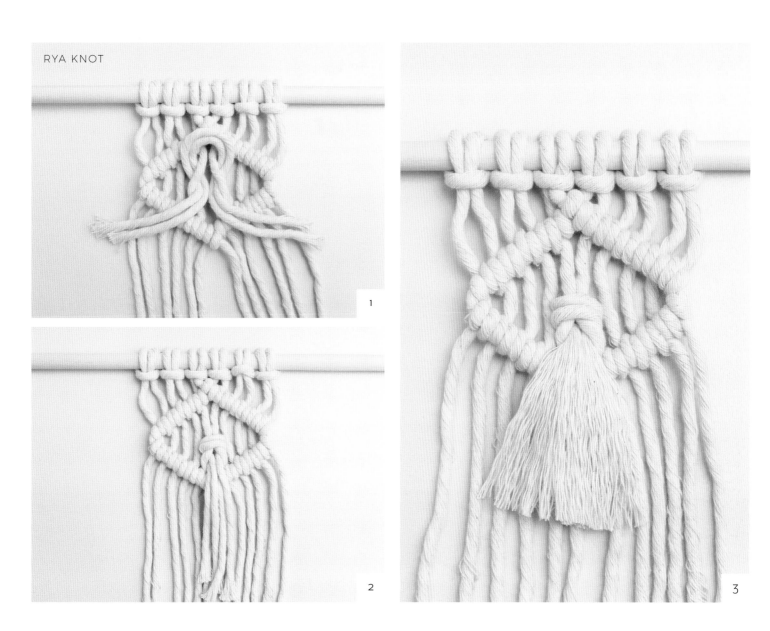

RYA KNOT (WEAVING TASSEL)

This tassel technique is used when weaving on a loom, but can also be tied on to 2 cords that have tension, and therefore works perfectly in some aspects of macramé.

1. Using a piece of rope or multiple strands of string, place its center horizontally across a pair of taut cords. Wrap the ends of your cord around the back and down through the center of the taut cords.

2. Pull the ends down and tight to stay in place.

3. Brush out and trim.

1

2

macramé patterns
SQUARE KNOT SINNET

This sinnet pattern is used a lot in classic plant hangers and in wall hanging designs.

1. Begin by tying a square knot (page 130).

2. Continue tying square knots on the same cords until you reach your desired length. Each individual square knot you tie consecutively increases the overall length of the sinnet. Be sure to tie each knot tight to each other, leaving minimal gaps so you don't see much of the filler cords. You can push up slightly on the knots if you are finding there are gaps in between. Do not tie 2 left-facing or right-facing half knots back-to-back because your piece will begin to twist (see Half Knot Sinnet, page 141).

HALF KNOT SINNET

1. Refer to the half knot instructions (page 129) and repeatedly tie the same left-facing half knots to your desired length. This creates a right-twisting sinnet.

2 Be sure to tie each knot tight to each other, leaving minimal gaps so you don't see much of the filler cords. You can slightly push up on the knots if you are finding there are gaps in between. Tie a left-twisting sinnet by tying only right-facing half knots.

1a

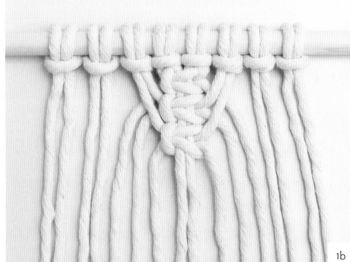

1b

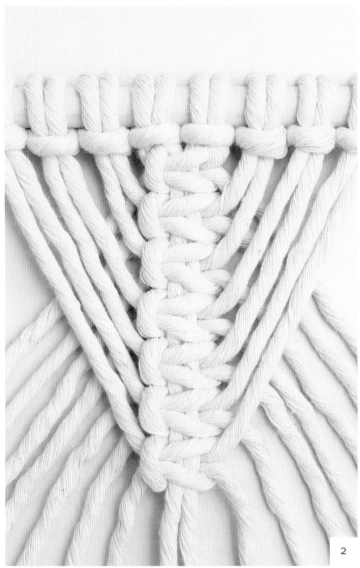

2

SQUARE KNOT SINNET WITH DIFFERENT WORKING CORDS (PINE TREE PATTERN)

When creating a pine tree pattern, you are continually using new working cords from a series of knots usually above where you are tying the pine tree sinnet. See photos for further clarification on which ropes to use. The new working cords you use are usually above and diagonal to where you are looking to tie the pine tree sinnet. To get the full effect of this pattern, continue this pattern by tying quite a few knots in the sinnet.

1. Tie square knots (page 130) as usual on the same filler cords, but use the next adjacent working cords for each square knot. Place the working cord behind or out of the way after tying each knot.

2. Continue to your desired length.

1

2

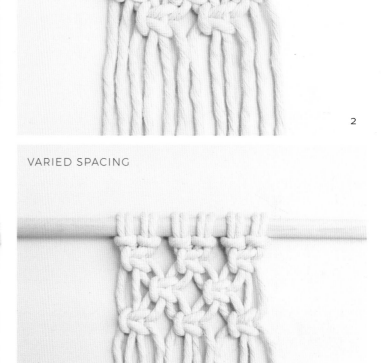

3

1

ALTERNATING SQUARE KNOT

This is one of the most common and simple patterns in macramé. It can be tied with or without space between each row. This changes the look of the pattern completely! Try experimenting with different spacing to vary the look.

1. For the first row, tie a square knot (page 130) with every 4 cords.

2. Excluding the first 2 and last 2 cords in the second row, tie a square knot with every 4 cords.

3. Repeat steps 1 and 2 until you reach your desired length.

VARIED SPACING

Here is an example of how different the same pattern looks by changing the space between the rows.

1. Repeat steps 1 to 3, leaving a consistent space in between each row.

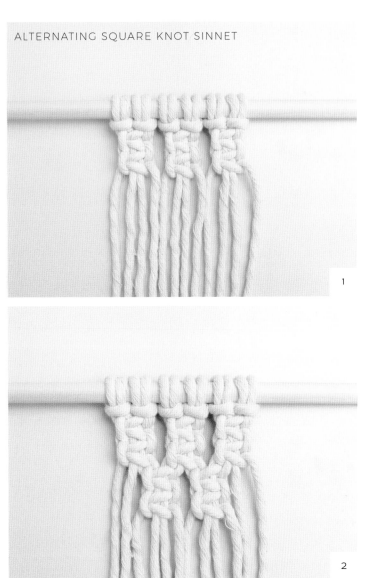

ALTERNATING SQUARE KNOT SINNET

You can tie an alternating pattern with many different knots and sinnets! To get more variety in your square knot sinnet patterns, try changing the number of knots you use in each row. For example, try tying 1 square knot in one row, and in the next tie 3 square or half knot sinnets and repeat that pattern. You can see this put into practice in the Ravana Plant Hanger (page 47).

1. For the first row, tie a square knot sinnet (page 140) consisting of 2 square knots with every 4 cords.

2. Skipping the first 2 and last 2 cords in the second row, tie a square knot sinnet consisting of 2 square knots, with every 4 cords.

3. Repeat steps 1 and 2 until you reach the desired length.

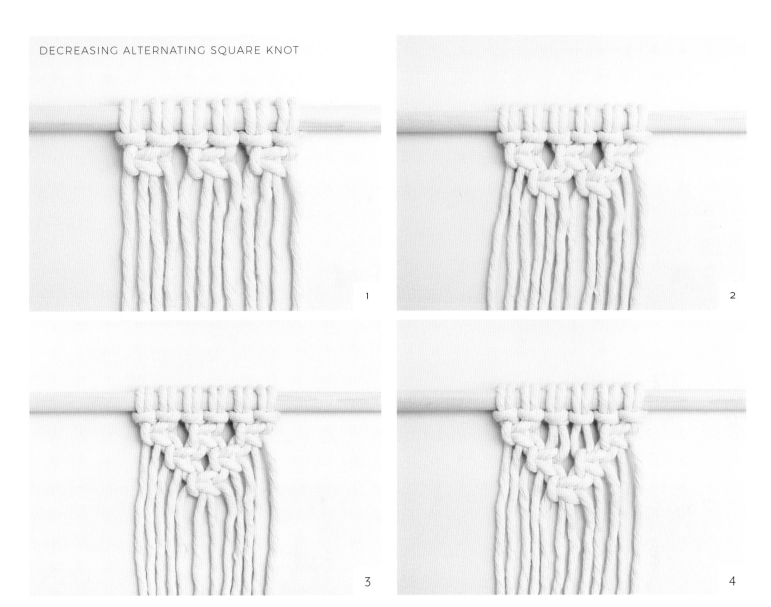

DECREASING ALTERNATING SQUARE KNOT

1. For the first row, tie a full row of square knots (page 130) with every 4 cords.

2. Excluding the first 2 and last 2 cords in the second row, tie a square knot with every 4 cords.

3. Exclude the first 4 and last 4 cords in the third row and tie a square knot.

Continue this same pattern with more cords to make a decreasing pattern larger.

4. To create the open version, tie square knots only on the outer ends of row 1.

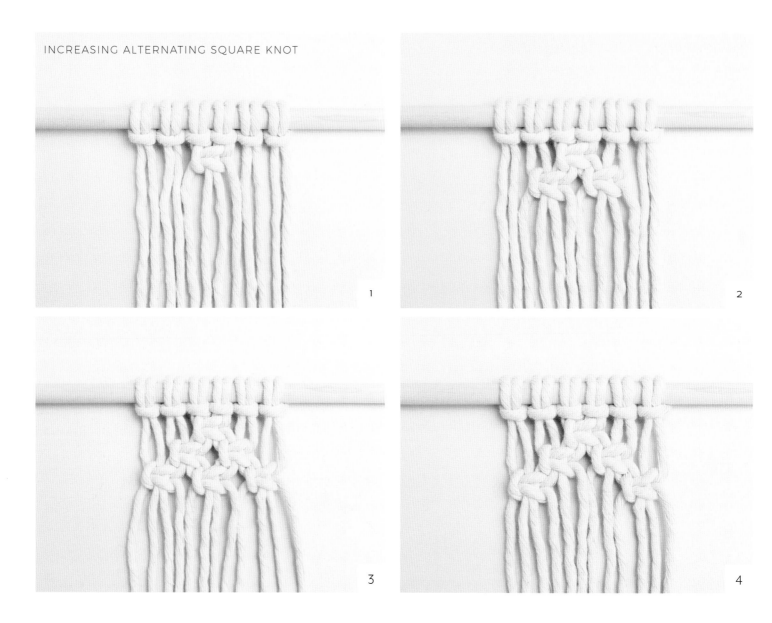

INCREASING ALTERNATING SQUARE KNOT

1. For the first row, tie a square knot (page 130) using the 4 cords in the middle.

2. Skipping the first 2 and last 2 cords in the second row, tie a square knot with every 4 cords.

3. Tie 1 full row of square knots across all of the cords. Continue the pattern with more cords to make the increasing pattern larger.

4. To create the open version, simply skip the middle square knot in row 3, only tying square knots on the outer ends.

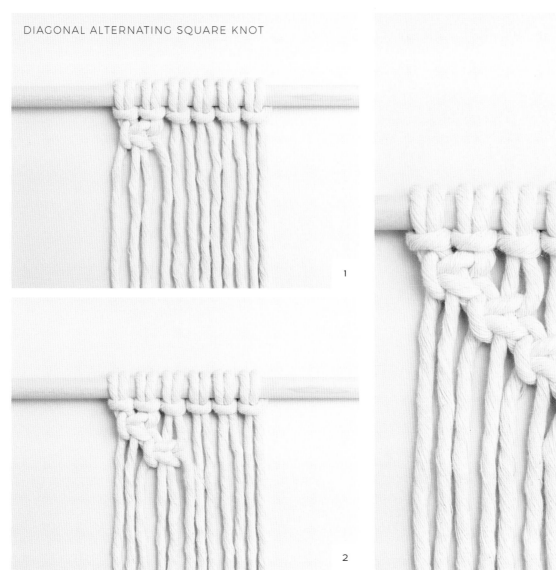

DIAGONAL ALTERNATING SQUARE KNOT

Also called a row of alternating square knots. With this technique you can vary the spacing between each knot. The tighter the spacing means the greater the angle and vice versa.

1. For the first row, tie a square knot (page 130) using the first 4 cords.

2. For the second row, skip the first 2 cords and tie a square knot with the next four cords, so this knot is offset by two cords.

3. For the third row, skip the first 4 cords and tie a square knot with the next 4 cords. This would be considered angling down and to the right. Continue the pattern with more cords to continue the line of knots or apply the same technique to tie down and to the left.

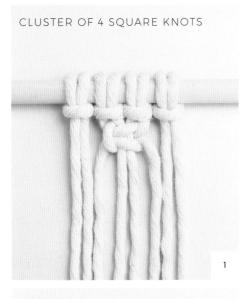

CLUSTER OF 4 SQUARE KNOTS

1

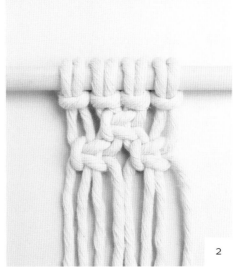

2

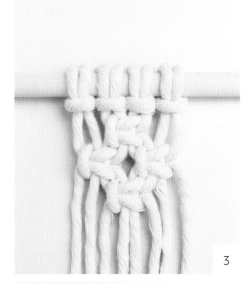

3

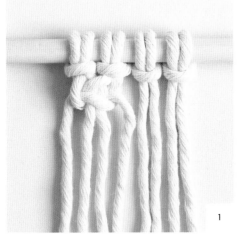

CLUSTER OF 3 SQUARE KNOTS

1

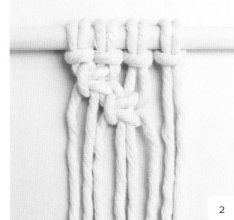

2

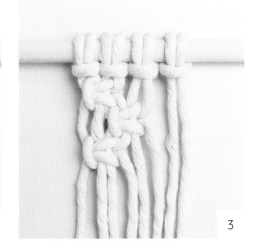

3

CLUSTER OF 4 SQUARE KNOTS (ALTERNATING SQUARE KNOTS)

This cluster can be done anywhere with a minimum of 8 cords; leave consistent space in between each row or tie them tight together. I like to use them as small accent knots within a project.

1. In the middle of the 8 cords, tie 1 square knot (page 130)

2. Tie 2 increasing alternating square knots (page 143) in the second row.

3. Tie 1 last square knot in the middle of the 8 cords.

CLUSTER OF 3 SQUARE KNOTS

I like using this cluster of square knots at the edge of a macramé piece. To tie this you need at least 6 cords.

1. With the first 4 cords, tie 1 square knot (page 130)

2. Tie 1 increasing alternating square knot (page 143) in the second row.

3. Tie 1 last square knot with the first 4 cords.

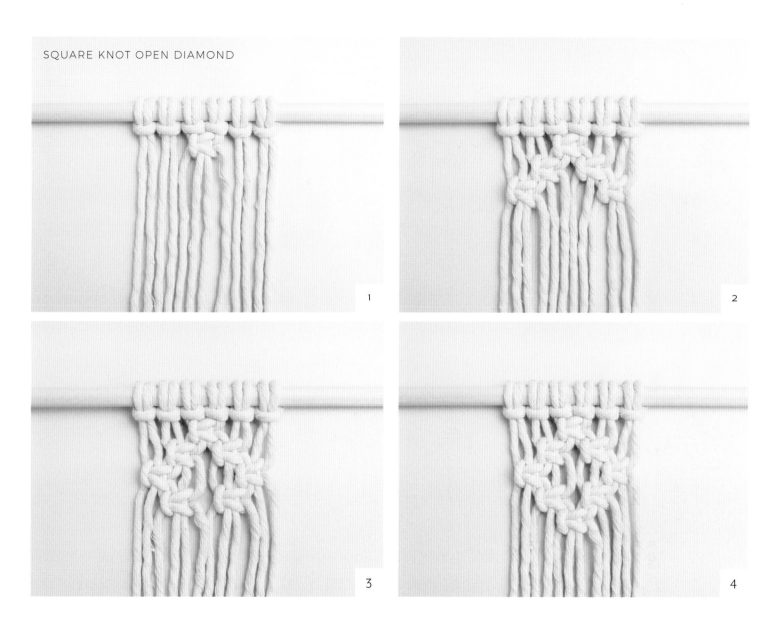

SQUARE KNOT OPEN DIAMOND

1. For the first row, starting with the 4 cords in the middle, tie 1 square knot (page 130).

2. Continue tying 1 row of increasing alternating square knots, open version (page 143), angling down and outwards until you reach your desired width or the edge on either side.

3. Continue tying 1 row of decreasing alternating square knots, open version (page 145), angling inward, until you reach the center of the diamond on each side.

4. Finish by tying 1 square knot in the middle of the cords.

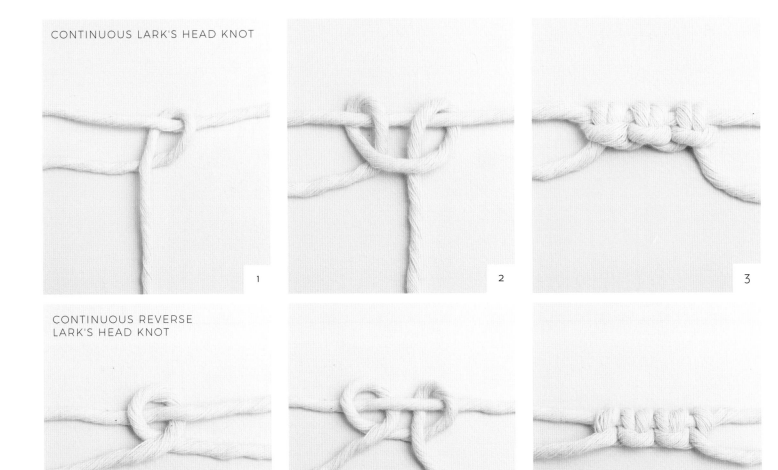

CONTINUOUS LARK'S HEAD KNOT

This can be done vertically or horizontally. This is helpful when you want to attach another layer to a project, or tie the knots close together for a standalone design. I incorporated this horizontally into a few projects in the book, for example to add on fringe on the Annalise Backdrop (page 89), Juniper Plant Hanger (page 55) and Harvest Headboard (page 15).

1. Using the working cord, wrap it in front of the filler cord and then back around the filler cord and around and on top of itself.

2. Wrap the working cord behind and then bring it forward around the filler cord, then pass it through the loop created by the working cord.

3. Pull tight and continue as many times as desired.

CONTINUOUS REVERSE LARK'S HEAD KNOT

This can also be done vertically or horizontally.

1. Using the working cord, wrap it behind the filler cord and then back around the filler cord and behind itself.

2. Wrap the working cord in front and then bring it behind and around the filler cord, then pass it through the loop created by the working cord.

3. Pull tight and continue as many times as desired.

DIAGONAL DOUBLE HALF HITCH

1

2

DOUBLE HALF HITCHES AROUND A RING
OR DOWEL

1

2

HORIZONTAL/DIAGONAL DOUBLE HALF HITCH (CLOVE HITCH)

When tying multiple rows of horizontal or diagonal double half hitches, you want them tight to each other with no space in between rows. After pulling the working cord around the filler cord, pull the cord away from you with some force (backward away from the piece); as you do this, you should see the knot move closer to the row above.

1. Hold your filler cord horizontally or diagonally at the angle you want it to be.

2. Tie double half hitches (page 132) continuously along the filler cord.

REVERSE DOUBLE HALF HITCH

The back of double half hitches are just as beautiful and textured as the front. The simplest way to tie reverse double half hitches is to simply flip your piece around and tie a regular double half hitch in the desired spot. Then flip your work back around to continue your pattern.

DOUBLE HALF HITCHES AROUND A RING OR DOWEL

1. I use this technique to secure the ends of the rope when wrapping around a ring. When tying double half hitches (page 132) around a ring or dowel, treat the ring or dowel as the filler cord and begin tying double half hitches around it starting from one side.

2. Continue tying double half hitches until you get to the end or your desired amount.

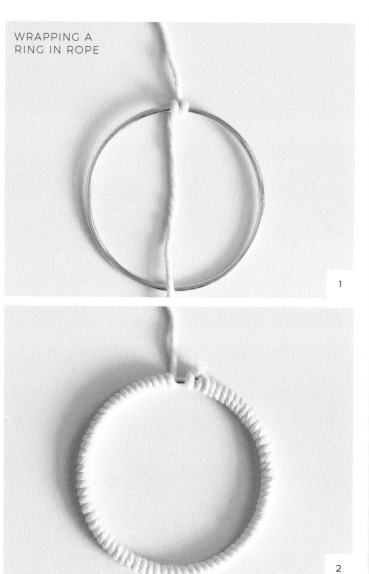

1

2

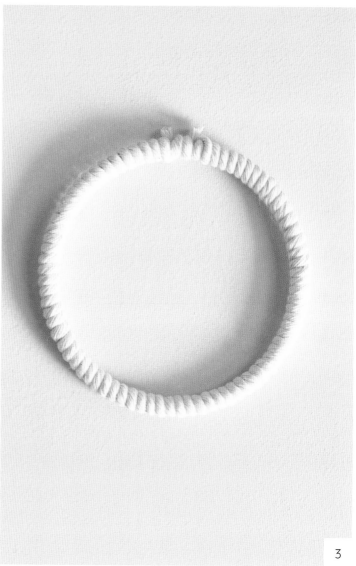

3

WRAPPING A RING IN ROPE

1. Start by tying 1 double half hitch around the dowel.

2. Wrap the ring completely until you have about ⅛ inch (3 mm) of ring showing.

3. Tie 1 more double half hitch around the ring to secure your wrap and cut the ends short. I try to cover these small knots under other knots when possible in a design.

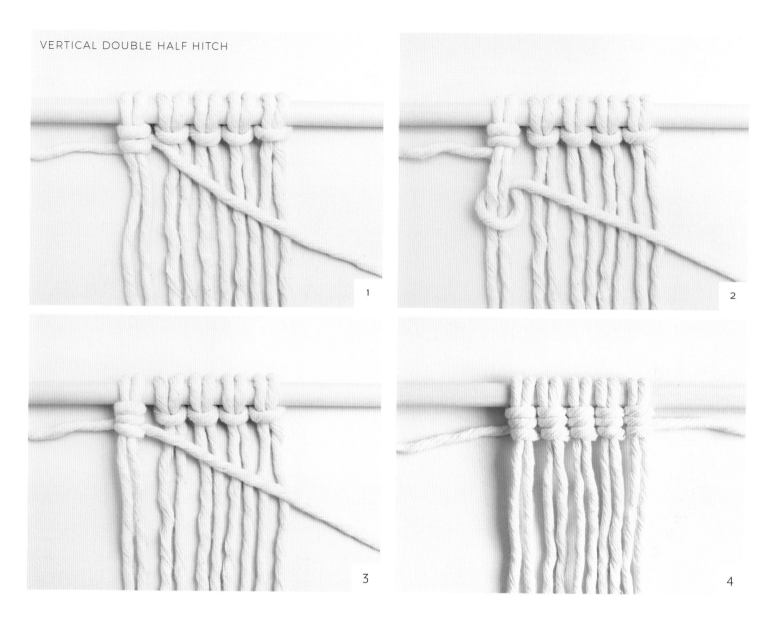

VERTICAL DOUBLE HALF HITCH

1. When tying a vertical double half hitch, the cords hanging vertically are your filler cords. With a separate cord, attach the working cord to the first filler cord by tying a half hitch (page 129). You can tie around 1 or more filler cords. I tied around 2 filler cords.

2. Make a double half hitch by tying a second half hitch on the same cord.

3. Pull tight to finish your double half hitch.

4. Wrap the working cord around and behind the next adjacent filler cords, and tie 1 double half hitch. Continue tying vertical double half hitches working left to right, tying one double half hitch on the filler cord(s).

Once you are at the end, begin working right to left beneath the row above.

DOUBLE HALF HITCH (FREE FLOATING)

I know this can seem a bit tricky, but you are really using the same technique when tying a vertical double half hitch. If you are having trouble, position the cords the way you would as if you were tying this knot in a wall hanging. I use this technique with the Dahlia Round Rug (page 65).

1. Tie a double half hitch around a single free-floating cord that is not attached to anything.

2. Pull tight.

Tip:

Each double half hitch knot listed above can be tied the way I like to tie them when working large scale to save time (page 133).

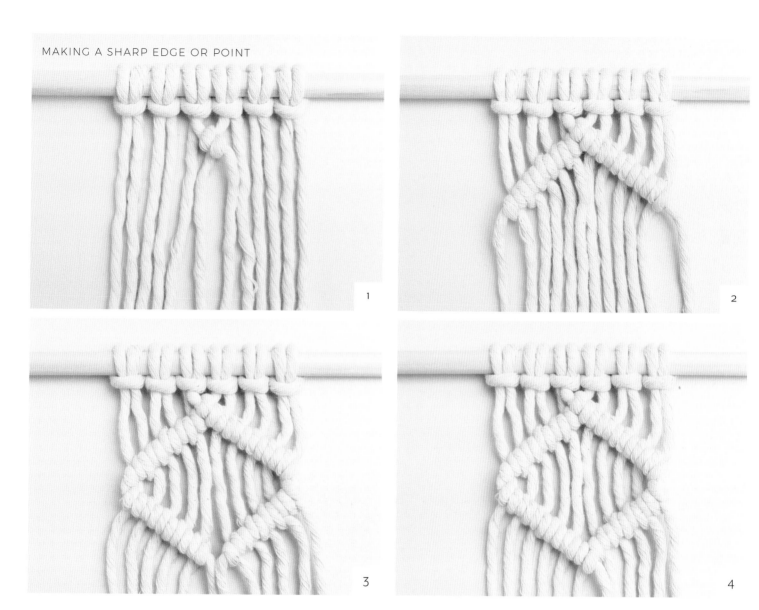

MAKING A SHARP EDGE OR POINT WITH DOUBLE HALF HITCHES

When tying double half hitches (page 132), sometimes you want your work to have a sharp edge or point to complete a diamond or V shape. This is how I tied the majority of my diamonds throughout the book.

WORKING FROM THE TOP

1. Start with the top of the diamond. With 2 cords, make one cord the working cord and tie it around the other cord using a double half hitch.

2. Now continue tying diagonal double half hitches (page 151) around both of the cords that you used to tie the double half hitch with from step 1. The first knot makes the point.

FINISHING THE BOTTOM

3. To finish the bottom of a diamond, tie diagonal double half hitches until you reach just the two filler cords in the middle.

4. Take the filler cord from one of the rows of double half hitches, make it the working cord and tie a double half hitch around the other filler cord tightly, leaving no space between the knots. This creates the point at the bottom, just like the top of the diamond.

1

2

3

4

5

DIAMOND OF DOUBLE HALF HITCHES

DIAMOND OF DOUBLE HALF HITCHES (CONNECTED)

You can tie a series of diagonal double half hitches (page 151) to form a diamond. This can be done with as many cords to make the diamond as large as you would like. For example, I used a total of 10 cords. This technique is used in the Riviere Headboard (page 27).

1. Tie 5 diagonal double half hitches angling down and to the left. From the first double half hitch, tie 4 diagonal double half hitches angling down and to the right.

2. Tie whatever accent knot you would like in the center of the diamond now. You could tie a macadamia knot (page 137), square knot with multiple filler cords (page 131), just a simple square knot (page 130) or whatever you can think of.

3. To close the diamond, start back on the left side. Using the same filler cord and angling it down and to the right, tie 4 diagonal double half hitches. On the right side, tie 5 diagonal double half hitches around the same filler cord, angling down and to the left. The fifth knot will join the base of the diamond together.

4. To tie another diamond under the previous one, start from your last double half hitch and continue using the same filler cord in the same direction, and tie 5 more diagonal double half hitches angling down and to the left. Starting back at the first double half hitch, tie 4 diagonal double half hitches angling down and to the right.

5. Repeat steps 2, 3 and 4 as many times as desired.

ACCENT KNOTS INSIDE
A DIAMOND PATTERN

SINGLE AND DOUBLE ARROW
DOUBLE HALF HITCH

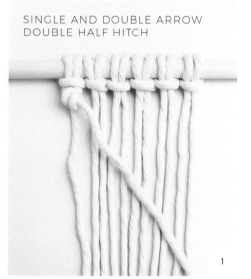

1

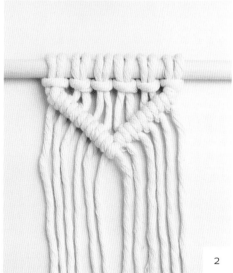

2

3

ACCENT KNOTS INSIDE A DIAMOND PATTERN

After tying a diamond from double half hitches or square knots, you can add different accent knots in the center of the diamond.

SINGLE AND DOUBLE ARROW DOUBLE HALF HITCH

To tie a single and double arrow, you are essentially tying a half diamond (page 155). When adding a second arrow below, use the same cords and tie it tight to the one above. This can be done with the point facing up or down.

1. With 2 cords on the left, make one cord the working cord and hold the filler cords down and to the right. Tie your working cord around the filler cord using a double half hitch.

2. Tie 4 more double half hitches and do the same with the same number of cords on the right, ending with a sharp point by using the filler cord from the right side as a working cord for the right side, or vice versa. This creates one arrow (or a half diamond).

3. Repeat these same steps right below your previous row. This creates a double arrow.

BUNDLING CORDS

1

2

3

MY METHOD FOR UNRAVELING ROPE

1

2

3

extra Techniques
BUNDLING CORDS

When you're working with cords that are extremely long, bundle them to make things easier. This helps keep your cords from getting knotted or tangled when you're working. It also makes working more efficient because you don't have to pull so many feet of rope through each knot.

1. Hold one end in your palm and tie a figure eight around your thumb and pinky finger until you reach the end.

2. Wrap the end of the cord around itself a couple of times and tuck the end into itself.

3. Pull tight.

MY METHOD FOR UNRAVELING ROPE

To get the look I like in my macramé pieces, I usually follow two steps when I am working with three-strand cotton rope.

1. Unravel the cords to your desired length/height. The cords will be very "kinky" after.

2. To make the fringe fuller and more frayed-looking, I unravel each of the three strands of rope by twisting it in the opposite direction the cords are naturally twisting, while holding the top with one hand. Then I carefully run my fingers through it until I reach the ends and carefully let go of the top, then the bottom.

3. Do these steps for all of the fringe for a nice full look. I have also found this to be the smoothest technique.

UNRAVELING FRINGE

If I have a relatively short fringe on a piece and I want it very unraveled, I use a wide-tooth comb and carefully comb through it after I've unraveled the three-strand rope. Make sure not to comb through it too aggressively, or you risk breaking the small fibers of rope that make up the strands.

I also like using a slicker brush because of its thin wire bristles. It brushes out single-strand rope perfectly, or 3-strand rope that has already been unraveled. Try to find one where the bristles are not too close together.

You could also use a fork! After unraveling the rope into its three "kinky" strands, hold the fork at a 45-degree angle and carefully brush through the bottom of the fringe. Don't use this technique any higher than 4 inches (10 cm) up from the base of the fringe, as it will end up making a mess of the small strands and knot up the ends.

UNEVEN ENDS

1. If you're at the end of your piece and your ropes aren't quite the same length, unravel them using "My Method for Unraveling Rope" (page 158).

2. The uneven ends will blend together. Alternatively, you can trim your fringe to the shortest piece of rope.

IF YOU RUN OUT OF CORD WHEN WORKING ON A PROJECT

If you happen to run out of cord while working, there are a few ways to add more cord. Whichever method you use, make sure you leave a long tail on both ends so that you can use a large-eye needle to sew the ends into the back of your work. The easiest and my favorite way to add more length is to essentially weave the new cord into the back of the previous knot, and continue knotting with the new cord.

MATERIALS/RESOURCE LIST

Here is a list of places you can buy your rope and other materials. Please note that I have not made purchases from all of these shops myself. Please do your due diligence before purchasing.

ROPE AND MATERIAL SUPPLIERS

CANADA
My website: Natalieranae.com
Ropeshop.ca (free Canada-wide shipping on orders over $100)
Etsy.com/ca/shop/BohoMontreal
Etsy.com/shop/macramebyJM
Etsy.com/ca/shop/lamaisondumacrame
Etsy.com/ca/shop/LotsofKnotsCanada

USA
Modernmacrame.com
Knotandrope.com
Knotstuff.com (email to place orders)
Etsy.com/shop/reformfibers
Niromastudio.com
Housesparrownesting.com
Rwrope.com
Bulkropes.com
Ganxxet.com
Hitchandcord.com
Etsy.com/shop/knottykatty
Holmmademacrame.myshopify.com

AUSTRALIA
Marymakerstudio.com.au
Edeneve.com.au
Familythreds.com
Stringharvest.com.au
Knotmodernmacrame.com
Jachomeheart.com.au
Etsy.com/au/shop/frayedknotsstudio

NEW ZEALAND
Etsy.com/shop/knottybloom

EUROPE
Etsy.com/shop/teddyandwool
Createaholic.se
Etsy.com/shop/miniswells

C-a-s-u-l-o.com
Miladruciarnia.pl
Etsy.com/shop/esmacrame
Clovercreationsuk.com
Loopsbylaura.com
Wooltheworld.de
Etsy.com/uk/shop/byyouworkshop
Creadoodle.com
Shop.bobbiny.com
Etsy.com/shop/mbcordas
Etsy.com/shop/cordilleria

ASIA
Ritzz.net
Yarnkart.com
Greendaun.com

MATERIALS SOURCE LIST

METAL HOOPS
Michaels.com
Joann.com
Createforless.com
Modernmacrame.com
Etsy.com/shop/allthememories
Darice.com
Amazon.com

WOOD RINGS
Michaels.com
Joann.com
Createforless.com
Etsy.com
(And some places that sell rope)

EMBROIDERY HOOPS
Michaels.com
Joann.com
Createforless.com

LARGE-EYE NEEDLES
Michaels.com
Joann.com
Createforless.com
Fabricland.com
Amazon.com

MILK CRATES
Amazon.com: Milk crates are great for conveniently cutting rope (see page 9)—I often also find used ones being recycled or at curbs

SHEARS
Amazon.com
Crescenttool.com: 2DAN 7¾-inch (20-cm) leverage shears

SLICKER BRUSH
Amazon.com
Your local pet store

WOOD
Homedepot.com
Your local lumber store/yard

LARGE SAWTOOTH METAL PICTURE HANGER PACK (WITH SMALL NAILS)
Homedepot.com
Your local hardware store

FABRIC GLUE (I USED ALEENE'S ORIGINAL TACKY GLUE SINCE IT'S ALL-PURPOSE AND NONTOXIC)
Walmart.com
Michaels.com

GORILLA GLUE (OR STRONG GLUE OF YOUR CHOICE FOR BONDING COTTON AND WOOD)
Homedepot.com
Walmart.com
Amazon.com

"RIGGA" CLOTHING RACK (ADJUSTABLE IN HEIGHT)
Ikea.com

S HOOKS
Amazon.com
(IKEA discontinued the S hooks I use)

SCREW EYES & HOOK SCREWS
Homedepot.com
Your local hardware store

ACKNOWLEDGMENTS

First and foremost, I need to thank my husband, Shawn. I don't know what I would do without him, and this book certainly wouldn't have happened without him. He stands by my side helping me through anything I decide to do. Shawn, your love and devotion mean so much and I couldn't have written this book without you.

Thank you to my family, who are always so supportive of anything I do and are understanding and continually pray for me.

Thank you to one of my best friends, Jenn (pictured below), who never ceases to amaze me with her talent and eye for photography. Thank you for letting me take over your home for a few months while we shot photos of all the projects; that was so kind and gracious of you and your kitties!

Thank you, Page Street Publishing, and Sarah, my editor, for trusting me with another book and bringing this idea to life!

And thank you God for the inspiration; my creativity, strength and passion come from you, and you alone.

A huge thank you to all of YOU who supported me with my first book and now my second. To all of you who follow me on Instagram, attend my workshops, purchase my macramé and rope! Your encouraging messages about my last book and the constant photos you send me of projects from my book always bring a smile to my face! Your support allows me to follow my dreams, and for that I'll always be grateful!

ABOUT THE AUTHOR

Natalie Ranae is a self-taught macramé artist, entrepreneur, educator and author who made her first plant hanger and didn't look back. She fell in love with the craft and made a career from it, teaching workshops, selling original designs on her website and creating large-scale custom orders for clients. Her first book, *Macramé at Home*, was published in 2018 to widespread praise from professional artists and amateur makers alike. Surrounded by her three cats in her home studio in Oshawa, Ontario, Natalie has created many large-scale pieces of macramé for individuals and businesses. From 16-foot (5-m) macramé feature walls in spas and wellness studios to window displays for stores like lululemon, she loves pushing the boundaries of macramé.

Graduating from OCAD University with a bachelor's degree in design, Natalie majored in and is also a professional jeweler and metalsmith. She has never limited herself to one form of creating and loves goldsmithing, knitting, crocheting, woodworking and whatever else she decides she wants to learn. Her unique approach to design and her attention to detail are consistent across any medium she works in. When she isn't making or working on growing her business, Natalie spends her time tackling DIYs with her husband on their 100-year-old house, volunteering locally and watering the jungle of plants in her home. Who says you can't be a cat and plant lady?!

You can find Natalie on Instagram at @natalie_ranae and on her website natalieranae.com. Tag her in your finished and in-process projects on Instagram!

Supporting small businesses and artists is important to her. Here are some whose works are seen throughout this book: Jennifer See Studios, Bethanie Kaye, East City Candles, Riki-Kay Middleton, Ash Timlin, Vintau Shop, KaeKoo Shop, SIN Ceramics & Home Goods, Lovt Studio and Mint Room Studios.

INDEX